southern plate

southern plate

CLASSIC COMFORT FOOD THAT MAKES EVERYONE FEEL LIKE FAMILY

CHRISTY JORDAN

with photography by jennifer davick

WM

WILLIAM MORROW

An Imprint of HarperCollinsPublishers

HarperCollins books may be purchased for educational, business, or sales promotional use. For information please write: Special Markets Department, HarperCollins Publishers, 10 East 53rd Street, New York, NY 10022.

FIRST EDITION

Designed by Mimi Dutta

Library of Congress Cataloging-in-Publication Data

Jordan, Christy.

Southern plate: classic comfort food that makes everyone feel like family / Christy Jordan.—1st ed.

p.   cm.

ISBN 978-0-06-199101-1

1. Cookery, American—Southern style.   I. Title.

TX715.2.S68J675   2010

641.5975—dc22   2010008684

11 12 13 14 DIX/RRD 10 9 8 7 6 5 4 3 2

This book is dedicated to everyone who came before me. Thank you for loving as hard as you worked, for passing down your wisdom in hopes of future generations benefiting from it (we have), for doing the right thing even though half the time no one noticed, and for knowing that the meals most worth eating aren't those garnished with sprigs of parsley or served on fine china, but those made by someone who loves you and eaten around a table filled with family and friends.

contents

introduction

I'll be the first one to tell you that I'm no one special, but I come from some awfully good people. In my opinion, some of the best people who ever walked this earth, and yet they were never known outside of their little boroughs until now.

No one would have known how my great-grandmother stayed up all night long on Christmas Eve, using ingredients she'd bartered for and squirreled away all year long so that she could make cakes for her children as their only gift on Christmas morning. No one would have known how a man who married my grandmother when my mother was thirteen years old would come to be known as the most cherished and loving grandfather I could have ever known, taking me under his wing when he was afraid I'd get lost in the birth order shuffle and openly declaring that I was to be his favorite.

No one would have known how my parents used to pretend to be busy in the kitchen while my brother and sister and I ate, waiting until we were done to eat what was left so that they could make sure our bellies were full.

Outside of our family, no one would have ever known these people were here—they didn't make much of an imprint on the world, I suppose, but they made every difference in the world to me and to all of my children and grandchildren to come.

No one would have ever known this were it not for the good folks who read Southern Plate.com, who have truly become my extended family.

A new member comes along and everyone scoots down and makes another seat at the table. I'm just the one lucky enough to get to fill the tea glasses and hug your necks as you walk out the door and go back to your lives.

My stories and recipes are a gift from my ancestors, but the ability to have them heard is a gift from you. Thank you for letting me bring them back again.

Gratefully,

Christy Jordan

southern plate

summer days
and family reunions

· · · · ·

nothing is more worthy of celebrating in the South than all of the family coming together as we do in the summer months. When I was a girl, we gathered at my Papa Reed's farm each summer for the Reed Family Reunion. Ladies would arrive in their Sunday best, toting casserole dishes, cakes, and plate after plate of deviled eggs. Papa Reed would hitch his big red tractor to a huge flatbed trailer and pull it up alongside the house. Ladies would then cover that trailer in tablecloths and bed sheets before setting out the spread.

The entire trailer would be filled to the brim, oftentimes having to rearrange plates just to make room for our bounty. Jugs of sweet tea and lemonade would sit near the end, along with a huge stack of sturdy paper plates. I tried not to be too obvious, but as everyone's head was bowed for grace, I'd look to see where Mama had set her mandarin orange cake and how close it was to the deviled eggs with "red stuff" sprinkled on top so that I could make my beeline to the two things I wanted most that day.

Afterward, folks would go back for seconds and thirds, many even fixing plates to take back home with them. Then we'd all sit in the front yard while the more talented among us brought out banjos and fiddles to entertain. Kids took turns swinging in Papa's rope swing that hung from the old oak tree out front of his workshop and the border collies made their way around, taking turns getting loved on by all the visitors on this special day.

No fancy restaurant could have possibly offered up food as delicious as what we had.

summer recipes

homemade banana pudding

I've always loved homemade banana pudding above just about all other desserts, but it took on a new meaning for me when I started Southern Plate. Mama used to make this and serve it up in her big avocado green mixing bowl. She'd let my sister and me layer the bananas and vanilla wafers when we were younger, giving us a butter knife to cut them with so we couldn't hurt ourselves, then she'd pour the thick pudding all over the top and let it sit a bit before supper so it had time to soak into all of the wafers. If we let her get it away from us long enough, she'd top it with a perfectly browned meringue. Oh my, it was heavenly.

Banana pudding was the first recipe I posted on my blog. I love to write and I love to cook, so the two came together when I decided to show folks who had never had "real" banana pudding how to make it. I took photos of every step, sprinkled it with instructions and commentary, posted it, and Southern Plate was born.

The key to the best meringue is to add the sugar while the meringue is still foamy to give it time to dissolve.

pudding

- 1 box vanilla wafers
- 5 bananas
- ½ cup sugar or Splenda
- ⅓ cup all-purpose flour
- ⅛ teaspoon salt
- 3 egg yolks (reserve the whites for the meringue)
- 2 cups milk
- ½ teaspoon vanilla extract

Place a layer of vanilla wafers in the bottom of a medium bowl. Slice a banana over the top. Repeat two more times with another layer of wafers and the remaining bananas.

In a saucepan (or double boiler; see Note), combine the sugar, flour, salt, egg yolks, and milk. Stir well with a wire whisk and place over medium-low heat. Cook, stirring constantly to prevent scorching, until thickened, about 15 minutes. Remove from the heat and stir in the vanilla. Immediately pour over the wafers and bananas. Let sit for 5 minutes or so to give the wafers time to absorb the pudding.

meringue

3 egg whites

¼ cup sugar

Preheat the oven to 325°F.

Make the meringue: In a large bowl, beat the egg whites with an electric mixer on high speed until foamy. Add the sugar and continue beating on high speed until soft peaks form. Pour onto the top of the pudding and spread to the edges to seal well. Bake for 15 minutes, or until the top is golden. Allow to cool completely before serving (refrigerate if you wish).

Note: Using a double boiler ensures that your custard won't scorch and is great if you want to be on the safe side. Having said that, I never use a double boiler. I just use a saucepan placed over medium-low heat and keep a close eye on it. I like to walk on the wild side that way.

8 servings

aunt sue's pound cake

Aunt Sue is famous for her pound cake, but not just because of how delicious it is. Everyone gets a smile on their face when Aunt Sue shows up toting her cake holder, but that smile turns to giggles as she sets the pound cake out before the meal. You see, Aunt Sue has a particular tradition that has been passed down from her mama—she lets you eat the crust off the top of the pound cake before she serves it.

Buttery and dense, this is a classic that is pure decadence served next to a gravy boat filled with Mama's Custard Sauce (recipe follows) over it. Do *not* preheat your oven for this recipe. Place the pound cake in the oven, and then turn it on.

6 eggs

1 cup (2 sticks) butter

3 cups sugar

3 cups all-purpose flour

1 cup whipping cream

1 teaspoon vanilla extract

Grease and flour a tube pan and set out the eggs and butter to come to room temperature.

In a large bowl, cream the butter and sugar until smooth. Add the eggs, one at time, beating for 1 minute after each addition. Sift the flour and add it to the creamed mixture alternately with the whipping cream. Mix until fully incorporated. Stir in the vanilla.

Pour into the tube pan and place in a cold oven. Turn the oven to 300°F and bake for 80 to 90 minutes, until a toothpick inserted in the center comes out clean. Cool completely before removing from the pan.

12 servings

mama's custard sauce

thank goodness for my mother—if Aunt Sue's pound cake is on the menu, she always makes sure this custard sauce is sitting right beside it. Rich and creamy, this is an old-fashioned sauce often used to pour over cakes. This recipe is hard to come by, as it is seldom written down, but rather passed through word of mouth as "a little bit of this and a little bit of that." I've had several people ask me how to make this sauce after the good souls who used to make it in their family passed on.

½ cup sugar
⅓ cup all-purpose flour
⅛ teaspoon salt
2½ cups milk
3 egg yolks
1 teaspoon vanilla extract

Combine the sugar, flour, and salt in a heavy medium saucepan. Whisk in the milk and place over medium heat. Cook, stirring constantly (see Note), until just hot.

In a small bowl, beat the egg yolks until smooth. Add about ½ cup of the hot milk mixture to the beaten eggs and stir. Pour the milk and egg mixture back into the saucepan and cook, stirring constantly over medium heat, until the custard begins to thicken. Remove from the heat and add the vanilla. Pour the custard through a strainer into a small pitcher. Cool, cover with plastic wrap, and refrigerate until ready to serve.

Note: I'm not kidding on the whole "stir constantly" thing here. Stirring prevents it from scorching, as it will easily do. This custard will seem like it's never going to thicken and then seems to do it all at once, so stay close and stir constantly! If this is your first time making custard, you might want to opt for cooking it over medium-low heat—it will take a little longer, but you'll have less of a chance of scorching.

2 cups

vanilla wafer cake

my mother got this recipe from her grandmother Mama Reed, and when she married my father, this was the first recipe she asked for to use in her own kitchen.

Mama Reed was known for her cakes and her large-scale baking. Of course, back then, they didn't think of it that way—she had ten kids, so small-scale baking was certainly out of the question. During the winter when family was expected to visit, Mama Reed would start baking cakes a few days ahead of time, and due to space constraints in the house, she'd set them out on tables on the screened-in porch covered in towels to keep for the few days until company arrived. This cake is sturdy but very moist and would no doubt have been carefully set out along with the best of them. My mother says this is a great cake to take to gatherings, as it is more stable than others, so it travels very well. It can also sit under a cake dome for several days and still stay moist. Trust me, the only way we know this is from the times Mama made more than one!

6 eggs

One 12-ounce box vanilla wafers, crushed (see Note)

1 cup sweetened flaked coconut

½ cup milk

2 cups sugar

1 cup chopped nuts (we use pecans)

Preheat the oven to 350°F and grease and flour a tube or Bundt pan.

In a large bowl, beat the eggs well. Mix the remaining ingredients into the eggs.

Pour the mixture into the tube or Bundt pan. Bake for 1 hour, or until a toothpick inserted in the center comes out clean. Let sit in the pan for 10 minutes, then turn out onto a plate. Allow to cool completely.

Note: An easy way to crush your vanilla wafers is to place half of the box at a time in a gallon zipper-seal bag and roll over them with a rolling pin or glass, then repeat with the other half.

12 servings

why your mama is
the best cook

every now and then a reader will respond to a recipe telling me it just isn't like their mother's. Sometimes they will go so far as to tell me I am doing something flat-out wrong because the recipe varies in some way from how their mama did it. It's these comments that stand out the most to me because my heart just aches for these folks. I understand there is a lot more to what they are saying than ingredients and preparation methods.

"It's not like Mama's" is not so much about missing the food as it is missing the person.

I feel the same way even though I am fortunate enough to still have my mother with me. She was the one who taught me how to cook, and as a result, I cook just exactly like she does. Anyone could taste a dish made by Mama next to one of mine and not be able to tell a bit of difference. Still, to me my cooking just isn't Mama's.

I want to make one thing as clear as possible: How your Mama made it is the right way. No one will ever cook for you like your mama did, and I'm surely not here to try. But on the other hand, when I bring you a recipe, I'm going to bring it to you how my mama made it, which is the only right way for me.

I know how much a mama can mean to a person, and I hope I can help bring back some of those memories from time to time, maybe by telling you a little of my childhood or my mother's childhood that reminds you of your own in some way. I hope that when this happens it brings a smile to your face, and most important, I hope that when you make a recipe of one of your loved ones it helps to bring a bit of their spirit into your kitchen again.

In the end, though, your mama will always be a better cook than you, me, Martha, or Julia. There was never any competition.

aunt looney's macaroni salad

macaroni salad is a staple at family gatherings and barbecues in the South. It's another one of those filling side dishes that can be made on the fly and with very little expense—our favorite kind. To get a Southern cook's macaroni salad recipe, you have to be quick, though, as I've never known one who actually measured anything out. Instead we make it by heart, adding a little of this and a little of that. My sister-in-law Tina, affectionately known as "Aunt Looney," makes a delicious salad, and I stood over her shoulder the last time we visited so I could bring you a recipe that would allow you to duplicate it. This tastes better if allowed to chill for several hours.

10 ounces dry macaroni

½ to ¾ cup mayonnaise (if you like more dressing, add the full amount)

1 tablespoon spicy brown mustard (you can use regular if you have it on hand)

One 4-ounce jar pimentos, drained

⅓ cup sweet pickle relish

Salt and pepper to taste (I start with ½ teaspoon of each)

Cook the macaroni according to the package directions. Drain in a colander and run cold water over it to cool.

Mix all the other ingredients together in a medium bowl. Add the macaroni and mix well, adding more mayonnaise if needed. Cover and chill. Stir before serving.

8 servings

mandarin orange cake

this has always been my favorite cake, although I don't remember Mama actually making it any time other than our yearly family reunion. She would make it three days before, set it at my eye level in the fridge (not sure if that was intentional or not), and keep it there, untouched, until the reunion day. It was pure torture.

Mama makes this a layer cake, but I prefer to make mine in a 9 x 13-inch pan for ease. I just frost it in the pan, cover it, and store it in the fridge until ready to serve. And if you don't lick the bowl after making that icing, I'm going to disown you!

cake

1 box yellow cake mix

One 11-ounce can mandarin oranges, undrained, diced

4 eggs

½ cup vegetable oil

Preheat the oven to 350°F and grease and flour three 9-inch round cake pans. In a large bowl, mix all the ingredients together well. Pour into the cake pans and bake for 30 minutes, or until a toothpick inserted in the center comes out clean. Allow to cool for 10 minutes in the pan before turning out to cool completely.

frosting

One 3.4-ounce box instant vanilla pudding mix

One 8-ounce can crushed pineapple, undrained

13 ounces whipped topping

In a large bowl, mix the pudding mix and pineapple together with a spoon. Fold in the whipped topping until well blended (this is going to take a lot of stirring, but hang in there). Frost the cake. Keep refrigerated before serving. It's best if made two or three days ahead and refrigerated before serving.

12 servings

Is It Homemade?

Is it homemade if I use a boxed mix? I get asked this question a lot and am always a little surprised. I answer it with a question: "Was it a cake when you paid for it at the grocery store?" Of course not—it was just a mix. You brought it to your home, added to it, and created a cake, so in my mind it's homemade!

Every now and then you might happen upon a stickler who will insist that your cake isn't homemade if you used a mix at all (which is ridiculous). My mother had a way of getting around this when she'd say, "Of course, I made it from scratch!" Then she'd add in a whisper, "Scratched my arm the whole time I made the thing."

seven-layer salad

every family reunion I've ever been to has featured at least one version of this salad. Granny Jordan loved to take this to church dinners. It's beautiful when layered in a clear glass punch bowl and it has always been a real crowd pleaser. I love its perfect blend of flavors and textures.

6 cups chopped lettuce

2 cups chopped tomatoes

2 cups sliced mushrooms

One 10-ounce package frozen green peas, thawed and drained

4 ounces mild cheddar cheese, cubed small

1 medium red onion, sliced into rings

2 cups mayonnaise

4 to 5 slices bacon, cooked and crumbled, optional

⅓ cup shredded cheddar cheese, optional

In a 2-quart serving bowl, layer the lettuce, tomatoes, mushrooms, peas, cubed cheese, and onion in that order. Spread the mayonnaise over the onion rings, sealing to the edge of the bowl.

Cover with plastic wrap and chill for several hours or overnight. Garnish with crumbled bacon and shredded cheese, if desired.

This salad looks great made in a clear glass dish so that you can see the layers. When serving, dip all the way to the bottom so that you get all the layers.

6 to 8 servings

jordan rolls

many old Southern families have a recipe for dinner rolls that they serve at gatherings and pass down to their kids. This is my special roll recipe. We love serving rolls with our meals, but they are especially good whenever you have ham, as they make the best little sandwiches for leftovers.

Make sure you have a warm place for your rolls to rise. Sometimes I turn my oven on 350°F for just 2 or 3 minutes, then turn it off and open the door to make sure it isn't hot but warm. Once it is just warm, I stick my pan of rolls inside for their second rising. Often in the summer, though, the garage makes a great place for dough to rise!

½ **cup sugar**

1½ **teaspoons salt**

5 **cups all-purpose flour, plus more for kneading**

2 **packages yeast**

½ **cup solid vegetable shortening**

2 **eggs**

½ **cup (1 stick) butter or margarine, melted, plus more for brushing**

1½ **cups warm water (like a baby's bath temperature—this is key in working with yeast)**

Place the sugar, salt, 2 cups of the flour, and the yeast in a large bowl. Cut in the shortening with a long-tined fork. Add the eggs, beating lightly with a fork before stirring them in. Add the remaining 3 cups flour, the melted butter, and warm water. Stir well. The mixture will look like a big old lumpy blob.

Cover with a dish towel and let sit in a warm place for 20 minutes.

Turn the dough out onto a floured surface. Sprinkle flour over the top and knead 3 or 4 times. Pat out into a square that is about ¾ inch thick. Cut into squares with a pizza cutter. Place in a greased 9 x 13-inch pan and cover with a dish towel. Let rise for another 20 minutes.

Preheat the oven to 350°F while the rolls are rising.

Place in the oven and bake for about 25 minutes, until the tops are golden. Remove from the oven and brush the hot rolls with melted butter.

approximately 2 dozen rolls

broccoli salad

as a child, I wasn't a fan of broccoli, or "baby trees," as Mama called it in hopes of winning me over. Growing up, I realized that it wasn't so much broccoli that I didn't like as it was cooked broccoli. This salad using fresh broccoli is one of my dearest favorites. I always make a double batch to send some to Mama because she loves it just as much. This salad stays fresh and delicious for several days in the refrigerator.

4 to 5 cups chopped broccoli

½ cup raisins

½ pound bacon, cooked and crumbled

1 chopped red onion

1 cup sunflower seeds

1 cup mayonnaise

½ cup sugar

½ cup white vinegar

Chop the broccoli, stalks and all, and place in a large bowl. Add the raisins, bacon, onion, and sunflower seeds.

In a medium bowl, whisk together the mayonnaise, sugar, and vinegar until the sugar is dissolved to make a dressing. Pour over the broccoli mixture. Stir to coat well and refrigerate until ready to serve.

6 to 8 servings

set an extra place
at the table

almost every memory I have of our dinner table growing up includes my mother, father, sister, brother, and at least one or two "extras." No matter how tight our grocery budget or schedule was, Mama always found time and managed to feed more people.

Usually it was a rookie police officer my dad was training. Sometimes it was a random uncle or bachelor friend of the family, and as we got older our own friends clamored into the mix as soon as they saw that a full supper at our house wasn't a special occasion but a daily event.

As we grew into teens, my brother had two friends who were brothers living on their own. After hearing them talk about pizza and not being able to cook, Mama invited them to supper one night. They ate at our table every night after for the next few years and none of us thought anything of it. Mama said that if anything ever happened to her, she hoped someone would do the same for us.

You don't hear about folks inviting others over to dinner as much these days. Instead, they'll take someone out to eat or meet them at a restaurant to share a meal, but in my mind the ultimate showing of graciousness and generosity is inviting someone to join you at your family table and dine on a meal cooked with your own hands. Inviting someone into your home is inviting someone into your heart.

It doesn't have to be fancy. Fancy food has its place, and it usually comes with a check. I never try to impress folks with my cooking by "gussying it up." An ideal meal for me would be a few vegetables, homemade rolls, and a meat—served on my every-

day dishes along with glasses of sweet tea. For dessert, I like to serve a pie or cobbler with whatever fruit I have on hand. I don't think twice about using paper napkins and my mismatched silverware, either. Come to my house and you won't get fancy and precise, but you will get warm and heartfelt. I just bet your home is the same.

So next time someone mentions "grabbing dinner" with you, why not open your home and heart to them instead? No matter what you'd pay at a fancy restaurant, the best dining experiences will always be priceless.

baked ham

even the smallest ham will feed a crowd, but I usually get the biggest one I can find so I'll have plenty for leftovers. Ham and biscuits make a great breakfast, as do ham and cheese omelets. At my house, whatever is left after a few days in the refrigerator gets chopped up, put in bags, and frozen to use in casseroles.

1 bone-in ham

1 cup pancake syrup

Preheat the oven to 350°F. Line a 2-inch-deep large pan with foil. Place the ham in the pan, and using a pastry brush, cover the ham with half of the syrup. Seal well with foil. Place in the oven and bake for 30 minutes per pound. Open the ham and brush with the remaining syrup. Leave the ham open and return to the oven for another 20 to 30 minutes to let the syrup form a glaze.

10 to 12 servings

"We're living high on the hog!"

Have you ever heard this phrase? It comes from the old folks who normally had to scrimp, but exclaimed with glee when they got to eat the best cuts of meat from a pig, which were located in the upper portions.

Nowadays this just means you're living comfortably or living the good life. Sometimes it is said in reference to a particularly good meal, as in "We're eating high on the hog today!" Baked ham is always a treat, doubly so if it's your mama who brings it, because then you get to take the ham bone back home. To this day, my mama usually has a ham bone in her freezer, just waiting to surprise us by using it to season a big old pot of pinto beans.

butterfinger cake

my sister-in-law Stacey is a great cook, even though she shunned cooking for quite some time after getting married. We didn't blame her one little bit, though, because my brother was a wonderful cook and he always hogged the kitchen.

The first thing most of us remember tasting of Stacey's was her Butterfinger cake, and as soon as she turned this one out we gave her little choice but to continue. Oh my goodness, is this ever good, and the perfect "wow" cake for any gathering. If you're going to a get-together or barbecue and want to bring the one thing everyone will rave about, take this cake.

1 box devil's food cake mix

One 14-ounce can sweetened condensed milk

One 12-ounce bottle caramel topping

12 ounces whipped topping

1 Butterfinger bar, crushed

Prepare the cake according to the package directions.

Immediately after removing the cake from the oven, poke several holes all over the top with a fork. Mix the sweetened condensed milk and caramel together and pour over the hot cake, spreading it over the entire cake. Cool completely, then chill well. After the cake has chilled completely, spread the whipped topping over the top and sprinkle the crushed Butterfinger bar on top.

12 servings

corn casserole

I don't know a single Southern family that doesn't serve some variation of this recipe. Although called a casserole and served as a side dish, it is breadlike in texture and I often serve cut squares of it as the bread to go along with meals at home. If you're a corn lover like me, you're in for a treat.

One 15-ounce can cream-style corn

One 11-ounce can whole kernel corn, drained

2 eggs

1 cup sour cream

One 8.5-ounce package Jiffy corn muffin mix (or another corn muffin mix)

½ cup (1 stick) butter, melted

1 cup shredded cheddar cheese

Preheat the oven to 350°F and grease a 9 x 13-inch casserole dish.

In a large bowl, combine the cream-style corn, whole kernel corn, eggs, sour cream, muffin mix, and butter.

Pour into the prepared casserole dish and bake for 30 minutes, or until lightly browned. Remove from the oven and sprinkle the cheese over the top. Return to the oven for 15 minutes, or until the center is firm.

6 to 8 servings

deviled eggs

every time I think of deviled eggs, I'm transformed back into a little girl with two blond ponytails and a sunburn streak down her part, peering over the table to glance over all of the options (everyone knows that big gatherings require more than one deviled egg plate) to spy my favorite, the ones with the "red stuff" on them. I had no idea what paprika was as a child, but I knew that out of all of the deviled eggs, the ones with "red stuff" on them were the best.

Deviled eggs are a must-have at any respectable Southern gathering, and don't you ever worry that someone else might show up with them as well, because I've never been to any reunion or picnic that didn't have at least two or three different trays of these little delicacies. This recipe comes from my Granny Davis.

6 to 7 eggs

Pinch of salt, plus more to taste

3 to 4 tablespoons mayonnaise

1 tablespoon mustard

1 to 2 tablespoons sweet pickle relish

Pepper to taste

Paprika, optional

Place the eggs in a pot and add enough water to cover by 1 inch. Add a pinch of salt. Place over medium to medium-high heat and bring to a boil. Remove from the heat, cover, and let sit for 15 minutes.

Place the pot under cold running water to cool the eggs. Carefully peel the eggs. Slice each egg in half and spoon out the yolk onto a separate plate. Add all the other ingredients to the yolks and mash with a fork until creamy and well blended. Spoon the contents into a plastic bag and seal. Cut off the corner and squeeze the mixture back into the egg halves. Sprinkle with paprika, if desired. Some people like to garnish with a slice of olive or a sprig of fresh herbs.

12 to 14 deviled eggs

How to Tell If an Egg Is Still Good

This is a handy little trick that has saved me from throwing out many a perfectly good egg. Fill a glass with water and gently place the egg inside. If it remains on the bottom, it will be fresh for a while yet. If it floats to the middle, you need to use it soon. If it floats all the way to the top, it needs to be thrown out.

fried chicken planks

it's hard to believe nowadays but there did exist a time before chicken nuggets or even chicken fingers. That made Mama practically a pioneer of innovation when she served up what she called "chicken planks" to us. They were one of our favorite meals, and to this day I haven't tasted a finer version of fried chicken. Of course, as with all of our family recipes, this one is pretty easy to make. Just don't go telling your company how easy it is!

Serve with Comeback Sauce (recipe follows).

Cooking oil
4 to 5 boneless chicken breasts
2 eggs
1 to 2 sleeves saltine crackers

Pour the oil in a large skillet to a depth of ¼ inch. Heat over medium heat while you prepare the chicken.

Place the chicken in a gallon zipper-seal bag and beat out until ¼ inch thick. (No matter how kind and docile you are, beating this relieves stress.) Crack the eggs into a bowl and beat with a fork (again with the beating thing). Crush the saltines and put in a separate bowl (you should have any hidden anger issues completely worked out by this point).

Cut each chicken breast into three strips and dip each piece first in the egg mixture, then in the cracker crumbs, being careful to coat completely. Drop each piece into the oil and cook, turning once, over medium to medium-high heat until browned on both sides. Drain on a paper towel–lined plate.

Note: All the chicken planks can be breaded before you start cooking them.

4 servings

comeback sauce

this is a good old classic perfect for dipping chicken in. It also goes great with fries, sandwiches, and vegetables. My cousin Cindy introduced me to this recipe several years ago, and it sounded so good that I made chicken planks that night just so we could try it. After one taste, my husband and I were hooked. I cannot imagine an easier sauce to whip up at the last minute! I know that with all that pepper you're thinking this is going to be hot, but it isn't at all. The pepper just adds flavor, not spice. My kids eat this sauce and love it.

½ **cup mayonnaise**

½ **cup ketchup**

1½ **tablespoons ground pepper**

Stir all the ingredients together in a bowl until well blended. The sauce can be served immediately but is best if refrigerated several hours.

1 cup

No One Is Born a Good Cook

No one is born a good cook. Despite what some people might lead you to believe, being able to cook is not some elusive talent that some have and others do not. It is a skill, easily acquired and easily mastered to whatever level you choose to take it.

All you need is the right recipe, answers to any questions you may have, and a little bit of confidence.

fried corn

lay out a table with every dish imaginable, absolutely everything under the sun, and if there is fresh fried corn on that table, you'll know where to find me.

There is nothing in this world like the flavor of fresh corn, shucked and cut off the cob and cooked up in a skillet. No matter how hard companies may try (and I do appreciate their efforts), no frozen or canned corn can even come close.

When we were little, shucking corn was a family affair. Mama would put a few buckets on the front porch and we'd each get our own brush and then everyone would set to work. We'd shuck a few bushels and she'd set to cutting it off the cob and cooking it up for everyone. I remember being able to have all the corn we wanted at dinner, but it seems now that I'm grown and have my own family, I can never have such bounty. No matter how much I make, we always want more.

Corn varies in starch content. If your corn is too thick after it cooks, add a little extra water. If it ends up too thin, mix together 1 tablespoon flour and ¼ cup warm water with a fork. Blend together well and stir into the corn. Cook for a few minutes more over low heat until thickened.

8 fresh ears of corn

2 tablespoons margarine

1 tablespoon bacon grease or vegetable oil

½ teaspoon salt, or to taste

¼ teaspoon pepper, or to taste

½ cup water, plus more if needed

Shuck and remove the silks from the corn (a stiff brush is good for removing the silks). Cut the kernels off the cob with a sharp knife, leaving about one quarter of the kernel. Scrape the cobs clean with the blade of the knife to get the pulp. Place the margarine and bacon grease in a skillet. Add the corn and corn pulp. Season with salt and pepper. Add the water.

Bring just to a boil, stirring constantly (corn scorches easily). Reduce the heat to a simmer and continue cooking, stirring, for about 30 minutes.

If putting this dish up for the freezer, just cook about halfway through and then cool and place in freezer bags or containers and label. Thaw when ready to use and cook for 30 minutes just as described above.

Mama likes to place her ear of corn in the center of an angel food cake pan and then cut the kernels off and scrape it down. The center of the pan helps hold the ear in place so that the kernels and scrapings fall right into the pan below.

6 to 8 servings

my first dinner party—
a love for corn gone wrong

I don't know what it is about corn that causes us—me in particular—to love it so much. I'll put corn in anything, and pretty much have. When I was about sixteen, my parents went out of town for the weekend. Of course, they wanted us to keep to ourselves, abide by the usual rules, and not have friends over. And I would have done just that, too, if I hadn't gotten it in my head that having my parents gone for the weekend was the perfect time to throw my very first dinner party.

At that point, I hadn't cooked a whole lot on my own—Mama or one of my grandmothers had always been right there beside me telling me what to do, but I knew how to make a mean spaghetti, and even then it was one of the most economical meals to feed a family. Now many of you are wondering at this point what on earth spaghetti has to do with corn. Hang on there—I go off on tangents, but eventually make my way round the bend again.

I invited five or six friends over to dinner and had my spaghetti sauce simmering nicely. After I set the table, though, I decided this meal was a little plain and needed some pizzazz. Having just finished my home economics course in high school, I knew that meals should have a variety of colors, and this one was all pasta and red. What to do? Add vegetables, of course! So I went through our freezer and found a bag of frozen okra and a bag of frozen corn. A few minutes later, I had a very colorful marinara sauce, which was met with some very strange-looking expressions as I served my guests later that evening.

To this day I still get teased about that meal—we all have a good laugh about the time I made spaghetti with okra and corn. Ahh, the enterprise of teenagers. Just goes to show that we all start somewhere.

granny's sheath cake

this cake has many names, depending on who makes it. I've often heard it called Texas sheath cake or chocolate sheath cake. We just call it Granny's sheath cake because our granny was the one who always made it. If you like a deeply moist chocolate cake experience with a decadent fudgy icing, pull up a fork and wait for the oven timer to go off.

I set the saucepan aside after making cake and use the same saucepan to make the icing. It saves having to wash the pan in between. This cake is served the same as a sheet cake, directly from the pan. The cinnamon gives it a wonderful flavor that people can't seem to figure out.

cake

- 2 cups granulated sugar
- 2 cups sifted all-purpose flour
- ½ cup (1 stick) margarine
- ½ cup shortening
- ¼ cup unsweetened cocoa powder
- 1 cup water
- ½ cup buttermilk
- 2 eggs, lightly beaten
- 1 teaspoon baking soda
- 1 teaspoon ground cinnamon
- 1 teaspoon vanilla extract

Preheat the oven to 400°F. Lightly grease a 9 x 13-inch pan. Sift the sugar and flour into a large bowl.

In a saucepan, combine the margarine, shortening, cocoa powder, and water. Place over medium-high heat and bring to a rapid boil, whisking to combine the ingredients. Remove from the heat, pour into the flour-sugar mixture, and stir.

Mix in the remaining ingredients and pour into the baking pan. Bake for 20 minutes, until the center springs back when lightly pressed. Five minutes before the cake is done, make the icing.

icing

- ½ cup (1 stick) margarine
- ¼ cup unsweetened cocoa powder
- 6 tablespoons milk
- One 1-pound box confectioners' sugar
- 1 teaspoon vanilla extract
- 1 cup chopped pecans, optional

Make the icing: In a medium saucepan over medium heat, bring the margarine, cocoa powder, and milk to a boil. Remove from the heat and add the confectioners' sugar and vanilla. Beat well with a whisk. Add the pecans and spread over the hot cake while still in the pan.

12 servings

cheesy hash brown casserole

in the South, we have two primary hash brown casseroles. They are both delicious in their own right, so of course I'm going to include both of them here so that you can pick your favorite. This is the cheesy one, which dethroned the sour creamy one as my favorites several years back.

Round these parts, a good hash brown casserole is required food not only at family reunions but at funerals, too. I'm not sure how family and friends handle funerals in other parts of the country, but below the Mason-Dixon Line, if someone passes on, folks get cooking to help out the family in their time of grief. So you'd best keep this recipe handy "jes in case someone up 'n dies on ya."

One 10.5-ounce can cream of chicken soup, undiluted

½ cup chopped onion

½ cup (1 stick) margarine or butter, melted

1 teaspoon salt

½ teaspoon black pepper

2 cups grated cheddar cheese

2 pounds frozen shredded hash brown potatoes, thawed

Preheat the oven to 350°F. In a large bowl, combine the soup, onion, melted butter, salt, and pepper and stir well. Stir in the cheese and frozen hash browns.

Place in a 9 x 13-inch dish and bake for 30 minutes, or until bubbly.

6 to 8 servings

sour cream hash brown casserole

this is the classic reunion casserole that everyone loves, young and old alike. My mother counts this as her all-time favorite.

This is one of the first "signature" recipes that Mama acquired. In fact, it's on page one in her personal recipe book—the one I hope to inherit someday.

One 2-pound package frozen cubed hash browns

One 16-ounce carton sour cream

One 10.75-ounce can cream of celery soup, undiluted

1 cup shredded cheddar cheese

⅓ cup margarine, melted

1 teaspoon salt

1 teaspoon coarsely ground black pepper

½ cup Ritz cracker crumbs

Preheat the oven to 350°F and grease a 9 x 13-inch casserole dish.

In a large bowl, combine all the ingredients except the cracker crumbs. Spoon into the casserole dish. Sprinkle the cracker crumbs evenly on top. Bake for 40 minutes, or until bubbly.

6 to 8 servings

strawberry pretzel salad

this salad sounds strange, I know, but it is nothing short of heavenly. Whenever we have it at a get-together, it's the first to go! Although the crust is made of pretzels, everyone thinks it's chopped pecans when they take a bite. I like to serve it with side dishes and call it a "salad," so folks can put it on their main plate and still have call for dessert. Southerners are clever that way.

2½ **cups crushed pretzels**

⅓ **cup margarine**

3 **tablespoons sugar**

One 8-ounce package cream cheese, at room temperature

1 **cup sugar or Splenda**

One 13-ounce carton frozen whipped topping, thawed

Two 3-ounce boxes strawberry gelatin (you can use sugar-free)

2 **cups boiling water**

Two 10-ounce packages frozen sliced sweetened strawberries

Preheat the oven to 350°F.

In a large bowl, mix the crushed pretzels, margarine, and 3 tablespoons sugar.

Press into the bottom of 9 x 13-inch ovenproof casserole dish. Bake for 10 minutes. Remove from the oven and cool completely.

In a separate large bowl, mix the cream cheese with 1 cup sugar; add the whipped topping and mix well. Spread over the cooled pretzel crust. Dissolve the gelatin in the boiling water; add the frozen strawberries. Break up the strawberries with a fork as they begin to thaw, while stirring. Chill until slightly thickened. Pour over the whipped topping layer. Chill until set. Cut into squares to serve.

12 servings

meme's mashed potatoes

I've never had mashed potatoes as delicious as my Grandmother Lucille's. The kids all call her "MeMe," and every time we serve mashed potatoes at a family meal, the question always arises, "Are these MeMe's mashed potatoes?" The adults know to get their plates fixed before this question is asked if at all possible because as soon as the kids find out that they are, they tend to disappear pretty quickly!

Grandmama actually uses a pressure cooker to make her potatoes extra-tender. I never use a pressure cooker myself, so I just cook the dickens out of them.

5 pounds mashed potatoes (or 7 to 8 medium potatoes)

1 teaspoon salt for the water

One 5-ounce can evaporated milk

½ cup (1 stick) margarine

1 teaspoon salt for the potatoes

½ teaspoon black pepper

Peel and cut the potatoes into slices or large cubes. Fill a large pot with enough water to cover the potatoes. Add 1 teaspoon salt. Add the potatoes, bring to a boil, and boil gently for about 30 minutes, until very tender. Drain the potatoes well and add the remaining ingredients. Mix with an electric mixer until smooth and creamy.

8 servings

perfect iced tea

if there is one thing Southerners are known for, it's our iced tea. We pretty much get weaned off of milk with it (I am not exaggerating here) and drink it at every meal save for breakfast (but even then it's entirely acceptable). When folks find out that I write about Southern food, the one thing I hear most often is "I just can't make good tea." So far, I've been able to remedy this each time because the mistake is a simple and common one—pouring hot water directly over your sugar. This scorches it and causes the tea to have a bitter flavor. The simple solution is to add a bit of cold water before pouring the hot tea in. Works every time!

5 tea bags

¾ cup sugar

Place the tea bags in a saucepan or coffee maker (down in the coffeepot). If using a coffeepot, run a cycle of water through to make tea. If using a saucepan, fill about 3 inches and bring just to a boil, then remove from the heat.

Fill a 2-quart pitcher halfway with cool water and add the sugar. Stir. Add the hot tea and stir. Add more water, if necessary, to make 2 quarts. Serve over ice.

2 quarts

lemonade

my mama makes the best lemonade! There is nothing like the perfect blend of sweet and tart on a summer day, but there is a trick to getting it just right: Heat the water and dissolve the sugar completely.

Whenever you see homemade lemonade in the South, it's usually served out of an old pickle jar and stirred with a stick. This is a staple in the South for summertime, along with iced tea. It is best served with a round lemon slice on the side of your glass.

1 cup water

1¾ cups sugar

1½ cups lemon juice

Combine the water and sugar in a medium saucepan and bring to a boil, whisking to dissolve the sugar. Remove from the heat and let cool. Pour into a 2-quart pitcher along with the lemon juice. Stir. Add enough water to make 2 quarts. Stir. Serve over ice. Refrigerate any leftovers.

2 quarts

Using Splenda and Sugar-Free Ingredients

I often use Splenda instead of sugar to lighten up some of my favorite recipes. I've found that if you use just a little less Splenda than what the recipe calls for in sugar, you can avoid the artificial sweetener taste. If a recipe calls for a cup of sugar, I scoop out a cup of Splenda and remove 1 to 2 tablespoons. Be sure not to pack Splenda—just scoop it into a measuring cup and keep it light and fluffy.

Each recipe listed below has additional instructions in the recipe itself on how to lighten it up a bit. Most of them just substitute Splenda for the sugar, but others have instructions for using lighter or sugar-free ingredients rather than the traditional method of preparation. There will still be some sugar, but with just a few simple substitutions, you can greatly reduce the amount.

- **Lucy's Chocolate Pie** (page 147)
- **Lucy's Fruit Salad** (page 164)
- **Depression Bread Pudding** (page 45)
- **Chocolate Gravy** (page 213)
- **Homemade Banana Pudding** (page 6)
- **Strawberry Pretzel Salad** (page 34)
- **Lemonade** (page 38)
- **Perfect Iced Tea** (page 37)
- **Analoyce's Buttermilk Congealed Salad** (page 66)
- **Watergate Salad** (page 218)
- **Mama Reed's Baked Rice Pudding** (page 250)

fruit cocktail cake

I love and adore this cake. This is another one of those long-ago recipes that we've been making in my family for as long as I can remember. It's a great way to satisfy my sweet tooth with a taste from the past.

Made from scratch, the ingredients are simple and the recipe itself is not fussy at all, a combination I enjoy when it's hot as can be outside and my two kids are feeling whiny! If you've never had fruit cocktail cake before, you cannot imagine how delicious it is. I especially enjoy it warm. Then again, I also enjoy it at room temperature . . . and cold . . . and . . . oh heck, I just love this cake any way you can give it to me. It has a unique and moist flavor, unlike anything you've ever had.

cake

2 cups self-rising flour

One 15-ounce can fruit cocktail

2 eggs

1 teaspoon vanilla extract

1½ cups sugar

Preheat the oven to 350°F and grease and flour a 9 x 13-inch pan.

In an electric mixer, mix all the ingredients and beat at low speed. Pour into the pan and bake for 45 minutes, or until a toothpick inserted in the center comes out clean.

sauce

½ cup (1 stick) margarine

1½ cups sweetened flaked coconut

1 cup sugar

1 teaspoon vanilla extract

1 cup evaporated milk

1 cup chopped pecans

While the cake is in the oven, make the sauce: Combine all the ingredients in a medium saucepan. Place over medium heat and bring to a boil, whisking to dissolve the margarine and sugar. Boil for 1 to 2 minutes, until the margarine and sugar are completely dissolved. Pour over the hot cake.

12 servings

sweet-and-sour green beans

the classic Southern meal is "a meat and three," meaning a meat and any three vegetables you can come up with, preferably from your garden. When green beans are in abundance, my grandmother fixes them up and puts them in her freezer. We look on a bowl of her green beans as one of the finest dishes that could be placed upon a table. When I can't have Grandmama's green beans, this is the only other way I'll eat them.

These green beans freeze very well. I like to make a triple batch and freeze leftovers in quart-sized bags to serve at another meal on a busy day.

½ **package bacon (6 or 7 slices)**

½ **onion, chopped**

32 **ounces French-style green beans (or other green beans)**

2 **tablespoons vinegar**

2 **tablespoons sugar**

Salt and pepper to taste

Cut the bacon into 1-inch segments. Place the bacon and onion in a skillet and cook over medium heat until browned, stirring often. Remove to a plate. Add the green beans to the bacon grease and continue cooking over medium heat until they are cooked to the desired tenderness. Add the vinegar and sugar and stir to dissolve the sugar.

Return the bacon and onions to the pan and simmer for 5 minutes, stirring often. Season with salt and pepper to taste. Serve warm.

4 to 6 servings

broccoli and cauliflower salad

my daddy is not a huge fan of salads, but this hearty and filling recipe is one he never refuses. It's best if made several hours ahead of time and stored in the refrigerator, where it keeps well for several days. This is one of those dishes that my mother seems to always have on hand. Mama leaves the onions out of this because she has never liked uncooked onions. On the flip side, I like raw onions so much I have been known to add extra.

1 head cauliflower, broken and sliced

1 head broccoli, cut up

2 small onions, cut and separated into rings

½ cup mayonnaise

⅓ cup vegetable oil

⅓ cup cider vinegar

¼ cup sugar

½ teaspoon salt

¼ teaspoon black pepper

Combine the vegetables in a large bowl. Whisk together the remaining ingredients in a separate bowl. Add the vegetables and toss to coat. Refrigerate until ready to serve.

6 to 8 servings

waste-not, want-not french toast

in the summer, I always seem to have a few leftover buns here and there. Rather than let them sit on the counter until they finally get thrown away, I whip up my kids' favorite French toast.

Now, the ingredients are surprising, but not nearly as surprising as the fact that this will likely make the best French toast you've ever had. The texture and flavor are wonderful, and what we don't eat that day, I place on wax paper–lined baking sheets and put in the freezer until hard. Once hard, I take them off, slip them into gallon-sized zipper-seal bags and return to the freezer. To reheat, just place a slice in the toaster on two cycles, turning after the first one (this may vary for your toaster).

Sure is lucky for me that frugality is in vogue right now. Well, it would be lucky if I cared all that much about being in vogue. . . .

2 eggs

¼ cup milk

1 teaspoon ground cinnamon

2 hamburger or hot dog buns

Syrup, for serving

In a shallow bowl, beat together all the ingredients except the buns with a fork until well blended. Dip in both sides of each bun.

Spray a large skillet with cooking spray and heat over medium heat. Place the buns in the skillet and cook for 3 to 4 minutes on each side, until browned.

Serve warm with syrup.

2 servings

depression bread pudding

this is a great recipe for leftover hamburger or hot dog buns and makes a delicious bread pudding. For all of you bread pudding lovers, this is quick and easy to throw together and can be made with Splenda instead of sugar. I often halve the recipe and mix up a little just for myself.

I have a more traditional bread pudding recipe using biscuits that you'll find on page 74.

4 hot dog or hamburger buns

2 cups sugar or Splenda

4 eggs

2 cups sweet milk (this is what old folks in the South call "whole milk")

2 teaspoons vanilla extract

4 tablespoons (½ stick) butter, melted

Cinnamon to taste, optional

Preheat the oven to 350°F.

Open the buns in half. Put in a 9 x 13-inch baking dish, brown side down.

Mix the remaining ingredients in a mixer and pour over the buns. Bake until the buns puff up and are heated through.

4 servings

Wasting Food

I hate to waste food. Now for those of you who have been reading Southern Plate for a while, I am likely sounding like a broken record on this point, but I can't help it—wasting food bothers me.

I've heard too many stories from my family about how scarce food has been in the past and children going hungry (in my family) to be able to take it for granted. I've mentioned this a few times before, but it bears repeating, as it is an issue that has impacted my life: I am the first generation in my family never to have known hunger.

This did not come easily—there were many times growing up when my parents would pretend they were busy while my brother, sister, and I ate so they could be sure we got enough, then they'd eat whatever was left. People have sacrificed so that I would never know hunger, and I'm not about to go willy-nilly tossing food in the trash when I can recycle it into something yummy with just a few added ingredients.

alabama white bbq sauce

this special sauce is pretty much unheard of outside of North Alabama. Even my husband from Georgia had never heard of white BBQ sauce.

This is truly a regional thing, and also a regional requirement. Every BBQ restaurant in North Alabama features white BBQ sauce on their menu, their meats, and their tables, and North Alabamians eat it with everything from french fries to bread to chicken and ribs. Its unique, tangy flavor is the perfect complement to just about everything.

2 cups mayonnaise

1½ tablespoons salt

2 tablespoons black pepper

6 tablespoons white vinegar

6 tablespoons lemon juice

¼ cup sugar

In a medium bowl, mix all the ingredients together and stir well to dissolve the sugar. Refrigerate several hours before serving.

2½ cups

number 5 bbq sauce

I spent two weeks developing my own barbecue sauce just before my brother opened up his barbecue restaurant. I mixed up different batches and stored them in mason jars in my refrigerator until someone could come by and taste them for me. Each jar had a number on top to correspond with my notes, and I bet my neighbors thought something awful funny was going on when I kept running out to meet cars in the driveway and pass off more mason jars for Mama and my brother to taste. The winner ended up being number five, the one I felt was just right. A few weeks later I was telling the story to my friend Shannon, and she explained that the designer Coco Chanel chose her famous perfume the same way, deciding on vial number 5 as the perfect one. I guess she never imagined her perfume would be considered in the same league as a barbecue sauce, but I find the parallel amusing. This is the first time I've shared this recipe—I hope you enjoy it.

½ **cup dark brown sugar**

½ **teaspoon salt**

¼ **teaspoon onion powder**

¼ **teaspoon garlic powder**

¼ **teaspoon chili powder**

¾ **tablespoon black pepper**

2 **tablespoons cornstarch**

1 **cup ketchup**

1 **cup water**

¾ **cup Golden Eagle or Yellow Label syrup (see Note)**

½ **cup cider vinegar**

1 **tablespoon Worcestershire sauce**

1½ **teaspoons white vinegar**

In a small bowl, mix all the dry ingredients. Place all the other ingredients in a large saucepan. Whisk in the dry mixture. Bring to a low boil, stirring constantly, then reduce the heat and simmer for 45 minutes.

It is very important that you mix the cornstarch with all the dry ingredients before adding to the wet ingredients. If you add it later, it will not dissolve completely and you will have little white dots in your sauce.

Note: If you can't find Golden Eagle or Yellow Label syrup, substitute ½ cup light corn syrup and ¼ cup honey.

3 cups

apple julep

living in the Bible belt, folks tend to make more nontraditional juleps without the alcohol. This one is refreshing and light, perfect for young and old alike. It's best served over chipped ice and drunk beneath a big old shade tree with friends.

1 **quart apple juice**

1 **cup pineapple juice**

1 **cup orange juice**

¼ **cup lemon juice**

Mix all the ingredients together in a large pitcher and serve over crushed ice.

6 servings

welcome to the south:
friendliness strictly enforced

the South is known for its hospitality. Folks here are said to be friendly, welcoming, and always ready with a kind word and a smile, eager to feed whoever happens by their doorstep.

But what most folks don't see is the flip side, that children born to Southern families will always be that way because, although we wouldn't have it any other way, we really weren't given any choice.

A perfect example of this is my very first driving lesson when I was fifteen years old, given by my Papa Reed.

We were riding the country roads near his farm, and I had a white-knuckle death grip on the wheel, nervous as a cat that I was going to accidentally run over into someone else's lane or have Papa and me lurching forward by pressing too hard on the brake pedal at one of the numerous stop signs.

All things considered, though, I was doing pretty good. We appeared to be on our side of the road (although old folks who veer into the other lane will just say that they pay taxes on both sides) and so far I'd managed to keep us both alive. Of course, when you start to gain that little bit of confidence, that is the prime time to be knocked flat on your face.

Out of the blue, Papa Reed's voice broke into my happy place and ordered, "Pull over. Right now." In all of my fifteen years, Papa had never used such a stern tone with me, and I panicked, thinking I surely must have hit someone for him to talk that way. I pulled over as quickly as I could without causing us to go off in the ditch while my eyes scanned the road looking for bodies.

Finding none, I turned to look at Papa, who was looking at me in a way that caused my blood to run cold. What on earth had I done wrong?

His next sentence brought it all back and I knew I had, in fact, committed a serious crime against the residents of Toney, Alabama. Apparently a farmer had driven by, and

in my earnest attempts to keep myself from having a head-on collision, I'd not paid any attention to the obligatory wave the driver had cast our way, and Papa, in his ill-laid confidence in me, had not waved back, feeling certain I would do so.

I'm not sure who was more embarrassed by my rookie breach of etiquette that day, Papa or I.

But his words drove it all home. "If you're too good to wave at somebody, you ain't got no right bein' on the road."

I've waved ever since.

texas caviar

this is truly the caviar of the South. With ingredients such as black-eyed peas, tomatoes, corn, and fresh green onions, what's a Southerner not to love? This keeps well for several days in the refrigerator and is actually better the next day, after the flavors have had time to blend.

Most folks eat this caviar with tortilla chips. Personally, I like to get a big old bowl of it and just eat it with a spoon.

2 cans black-eyed peas (with jalapeño if available)

One 29-ounce can petite diced tomatoes

Two 15-ounce cans whole kernel corn

¼ cup chopped fresh parsley

2 green onions, sliced

One 16-ounce bottle zesty Italian dressing

Drain the peas, tomatoes, and corn cans well and pour the contents into a large bowl or dishpan. Add the chopped parsley and onions. Pour the dressing over all and stir well.

Cover and refrigerate until ready to serve. Serve with tortilla or corn chips.

6 to 8 servings

vegetable salad

this marinated vegetable salad is best made a day in advance and stored in the refrigerator. It makes a wonderful side dish to any barbecue, and I like it so much I usually forego the main course and eat nothing else!

¾ cup white vinegar

½ cup vegetable oil

1 cup sugar

1 teaspoon salt

1 teaspoon black pepper

One 15-ounce can English peas, drained

1 cup diced celery

One 2-ounce jar diced pimentos, drained

One 14.5-ounce can French-style green beans, drained

Two 11-ounce cans shoepeg corn, drained

1 cup diced green bell pepper

1 cup chopped onion

Combine the vinegar, oil, sugar, salt, and pepper in a small saucepan and bring to a boil over medium-high heat, stirring until the sugar dissolves. Remove from the heat and cool.

Combine the remaining ingredients in a large bowl and stir in the vinegar mixture. Cover and chill for 8 hours. Drain the liquid before serving.

8 servings

fried potatoes

there aren't many cultures that haven't, at one time or another, relied upon potatoes as a staple in their diet due to their availability, adaptability, taste, and tendency to be very filling. Southerners, of course, are no different. I remember my great-grandmother Lela telling about how she used to pick cotton in the fields with her kids and they would walk back to the house at lunchtime and dig up some potatoes to fry for lunch. It's hard to hear things like that and not look at this bowl of potatoes as a connection to your ancestors.

¼ **cup vegetable oil**

6 medium potatoes, peeled and cubed (about 2 cups)

Salt and pepper to taste

In a large skillet, heat the oil over medium heat. Add the potatoes and salt and pepper to taste. Stir. Cover and cook, stirring occasionally, until browned and tender, about 30 minutes.

4 servings

okra and tomatoes

*this is **a great throw-together side dish*** when the garden is coming in, but I make it year-round with frozen okra and diced tomatoes. Sometimes I like to throw a little dry macaroni in to soak up a bit of the juice, but the best way to eat it is with a slice of warm cornbread.

1 cup chopped Vidalia onions (see Note)

One 14-ounce can diced tomatoes, undrained

2½ cups frozen sliced okra

1 tablespoon lemon juice

Salt and pepper to taste

Place the onions, tomatoes, and okra in a saucepan. Cover and cook over medium heat until the okra and onions are tender. Add the lemon juice and salt and pepper to taste.

Note: If Vidalia onions are not available, substitute any sweet onion.

4 to 6 servings

ms. millie's best coleslaw

Miss Millie is my grandmother Lucille's oldest and dearest friend. I consider her an adopted grandmother myself. She is kindhearted and as loving as the day is long, always ready with a word of wisdom or encouragement to anyone who needs it. We love her slaw almost as much as we love her.

Mama serves this whenever we have pulled pork barbecue alongside my grandmother's potato salad (page 197), and everyone who has it always requests it whenever they come back.

1 **medium head green cabbage, cored and shredded**

2 **medium carrots, peeled and grated**

1 **green bell pepper, cored, seeded, and diced**

2 **tablespoons grated onion**

2 **cups mayonnaise**

¾ **cup sugar**

¼ **cup cider vinegar**

2 **tablespoons celery seeds**

1 **teaspoon salt**

⅛ **teaspoon black pepper**

¼ **cup Dijon mustard**

Place the cabbage, carrots, green pepper, and onion in a large bowl. In another bowl, mix together all the remaining ingredients, stirring to dissolve the sugar. Pour over the vegetables and toss well to combine. Cover and refrigerate for 3 to 4 hours before serving for the flavors to blend.

8 servings

where do all of these recipes come from?

I had thirteen living grandparents when I was born. That number astounds some people and causes skeptical looks from others. For me, it was just a way of life. All of my grandparents were divorced and remarried long before I was born. It was as if they had all arrived at a dance one day and collectively decided they didn't want to dance with the one that brung 'em.

I came along several years after the dust had settled around their now-happy unions, and nothing seemed the least bit peculiar about such an abundance of guardians for one small child.

The strangest thing to most people is the fact that not a single one of my relatives lived outside of Alabama. My mama says, "Southerners just stay put, Christy." I was born in Huntsville, Alabama, to a mother who was born in Huntsville, Alabama, as was her mother before her. I lived my entire life surrounded by a slew of cousins, aunts, uncles, and my wealth of grandparents.

From them, I learned many things about life: how to jump rope, how to whistle, how to shake the tree so just the right number of pears fell into my sister's arms, and how to look at the world through the eyes of someone looking back and seeing all of the wonder that life has given them. My people were never wealthy on either side of the fence. They were poor people who lived hard lives but managed to be grateful for the day given to them at the rising of each new sun.

What do you get with a large family with roots this deep? As far as this Southern cook is concerned, one heck of a recipe collection.

Later on in life, when I decided to get my Home Economics degree, I knew these were the recipes I'd go back to rather than the fancier ones I picked up in college. Having lived all of my life surrounded by great home cooks, a good old-fashioned home cook is just what I set out to be.

hot dog chili sauce

I can't help it, I love hot dogs. But to gussy them up a bit, I add my daddy's hot dog chili. This is one of those recipes you get told over the phone whenever you need it and no one actually bothers to write it down. After calling Mama every time I wanted to make it for a refresher course, I finally got around to writing the recipe down so I could share it with y'all.

The great thing about this chili is that it freezes well. I like to make a double batch and freeze it in smaller portions to have hot dog chili all summer long. Hey, it's a double meat on a bun, how can you go wrong?

3 **pounds ground beef**

6 **tablespoons chili powder**

1 **tablespoon salt, or to taste**

1 **tablespoon black pepper, or to taste**

Place enough water in a pot to cover your beef. Take handfuls of the beef and submerge in the water, smooshing it up with your hands. Add the seasonings and stir. Bring to a boil over medium-high heat, then reduce the heat and boil gently for about 1 hour. Using a ladle, remove the grease from the top and discard. Remove the chili with a slotted spoon to put on hot dogs. Freeze leftovers for your next cookout!

12 servings

peanut butter balls

peanut butter balls were a staple in our school lunchrooms. Word got around fast on the day the lunch ladies were making them, and we all looked forward to the single serving we got on our trays come noon meal. Single serving for everyone but my brother.

My brother, who never once passed up a chance to be unusually cruel to me, managed to singlehandedly wrap every one of those lunch ladies around his little finger. While we all surfaced with our single peanut butter ball, Bill waltzed to his table with at least three.

This is a great snack for children and grown-ups alike. I store them in zipper-seal bags in the freezer and I often see my husband or son coming back from the freezer with a handful at a time. Full of all sorts of goodness, it's one snack that will not only tide your family over until you can finish up supper, but one you can feel good about letting them have. If my brother shows up, make sure to only let him have one.

2 cups honey or corn syrup
3 cups creamy peanut butter
5 cups dry milk powder
6 cups quick-cooking oats

In a large bowl, mix all the ingredients together with a hand mixer. Form into balls with your hands or a cookie dough scoop and freeze on wax paper–lined cookie sheets until hardened. Store in the freezer in zipper-seal bags.

approximately 100 balls

analoyce's buttermilk congealed salad

very popular in the South, buttermilk congealed salad is a treat that used to be available only in the winter due to our summer heat. We proudly serve this on the hottest of days thanks to modern conveniences. You can easily alter the flavor and color simply by using your favorite gelatin.

One 20-ounce can crushed pineapple

2 small boxes gelatin (your flavor choice; you can use sugar-free)

2 cups buttermilk

8 ounces whipped topping

In a medium saucepan, bring the pineapple in its juice to a boil. Add the gelatin and mix well.

Remove from heat, pour into a bowl, and stir in the buttermilk. Stir in the whipped topping. Cover and refrigerate for several hours before serving.

8 servings

dishpan cookies

as a girl, my mother made fresh homemade cookies twice a week, every week. She didn't realize how long cookies would keep, so she made small batches and replenished them with fresh batches every three days or so. Seeing as how money was so tight with a family of five on a police officer's salary, Mama kept the cookies coming because she didn't want us to do without treats when we couldn't afford store-bought ones. If you ask me, folks eating store-bought cookies weren't getting nearly the treat we were.

A very old-fashioned-tasting cookie, this reminds me of something I had in our lunchroom at school as a child. They get their name from the fact that the ingredients take up so much space, folks just mix them up in a big old dishpan instead of a bowl.

These are a great cookie to give away. They travel well, freeze well, stay fresh longer than most cookies just sealed in a jar on the counter, and they also mail well. Even better, if you like crisp cookies, just bake them 2 minutes or so longer and you'll have them crispy, too.

2 cups light brown sugar

1 cup granulated sugar

2 teaspoons vanilla extract

2 cups vegetable oil

4 eggs

4 cups all-purpose flour

2 teaspoons baking soda

1 teaspoon salt

1½ cups quick-cooking oats

4 cups corn flakes

Preheat the oven to 375°F.

In a very large bowl or dishpan, cream the sugars, vanilla, oil, and eggs. Add the flour, baking soda, and salt. Fold in the oats and corn flakes.

Drop by ¼ measuring cup amounts onto ungreased cookie sheets. This batter might be a little dry and you may have to smoosh it together with your hands to get it into a ball when you put it onto the pan.

Bake for 10 to 12 minutes, until the edges are lightly browned. If you want them to be chewy, bake a little less, crispy, a little more. I always double this recipe and do half chewy, half crunchy. They keep really well and are great for breakfast.

3 dozen

blackberry cobbler

this is one of those super-simple recipes from the old days. Folks seemed to really under-stand the value of "simple" back then, and I think it allowed cooks more time to put love into their dishes. Back then you knew what you were gonna make and then you walked into the kitchen and made it from the heart, without even having to look at a recipe. All that time agonizing over complicated instructions was spent instead think-ing of how happy Junior was gonna be when he came home from school and found you'd made the family's favorite cobbler. Thoughts like that just naturally make a body smile, don't they?

I really don't understand the thinking behind complicating things, but I know folks who prefer more complicated and sophisticated cooking likely look down their nose at my ways. You know what? I'm perfectly okay with that. I'm a *whatever-cranks-yer-tractor* kinda gal anyway.

This is my favorite cobbler recipe, and it comes out buttery and delicious. You can substitute your favorite berries in it and it will be every bit as good. This is also good with peaches—frozen, fresh, or canned.

½ cup (1 stick) plus 1 tablespoon butter or margarine

2 cups blackberries, frozen or fresh

1½ cups plus 1 tablespoon sugar

1 cup self-rising flour

1 cup sugar

1 cup milk

Preheat the oven to 350°F.

Melt the stick of butter in an ovenproof casserole dish in the oven while mixing the ingredients.

Place 1 tablespoon butter on top of the berries in a small bowl. Pour ½ cup of the sugar over the berries. Stir. Heat in the microwave for 1 minute so that the sugar begins to melt.

In a large bowl, mix together the flour and 1 cup sugar until blended. Pour in the milk and mix until blended.

After the butter is melted, take the casserole out of the oven and pour the batter on top of the melted butter. Pour the berries on top of the batter. *Do not stir!* Sprinkle a tablespoon of sugar over the cobbler. Place in the oven and cook for 55 minutes, or until golden.

8 servings

the cooler
days of fall

· · · · ·

fall is a time of regeneration for Southerners. With the sweltering heat of summer past, folks seem to get energized and in the kitchen once more, canning up the remainders of our garden produce and preparing for the holidays. Being the seasonal eaters that we are, a great many of our recipes make use of the incoming apple crop.

Although our winters are short, we enjoy them by cooking warm and comforting foods. Soups, stews, and spicy dishes abound, along with filling casseroles and baked treats. Many families plan gatherings at homes or churches, and some of the very best outdoor festivals take place during this time as well. Chili cook-offs, potlucks, and boiled peanuts take on a starring role.

I love all of the seasons in my beautiful homeland, but as far as food is concerned, I look forward to fall more than any other!

fall recipes

old-fashioned bread pudding

this is one of the most delicious bread puddings I've ever had and it's truly Southern in that it uses leftover buttermilk biscuits as the base. If you'd like, though, you can make frozen Southern-style biscuits and crumble those up instead. I love to serve this hot from the oven with a scoop of vanilla bean ice cream.

2 cups crumbled leftover biscuits

¾ cup sweetened flaked coconut

½ cup raisins

4 cups milk

2 eggs

¾ cup sugar

¼ teaspoon salt

¼ teaspoon ground cinnamon

1 teaspoon vanilla extract

Preheat the oven to 350°F and grease a 2-quart ovenproof casserole dish.

Layer one third of the crumbled biscuits, half of the coconut, half of the raisins, one third of the crumbled biscuits, and the remaining coconut and raisins in that order. End with the remaining crumbled biscuits. In a large bowl, mix all the other ingredients together, reserving 2 tablespoons sugar. Pour over the biscuits. Sprinkle the 2 tablespoons sugar over the top and bake for 1 hour. Serve hot with ice cream.

8 servings

did you know that you can freeze apples?

my grandmother Cornetha taught my mother how to freeze apples when she was a little girl. This is an old-fashioned method that preserves not only the flavor but appearance as well—and it's super-easy! Frozen apples can be taken directly from the freezer and used in any type of baked good, just like fresh apples. So pick them or buy them up in season and reap the benefits of your efforts well into winter. And don't worry, they won't taste salty.

1 gallon water
¼ cup salt
5 pounds apples

Warm 1 cup of the water and place in a large bowl. Stir in the salt until dissolved. Add the remaining water (cold). Peel and slice the apples (you can leave the skin on them if desired). Place each slice in salt water as you go along. When done with all the apples, stir the water a bit to make sure all have been submerged. Drain in a colander. Immediately place in freezer bags, label, and freeze.

southern plate apple fritters

my first memories of apple fritters come from a family trip to the Smoky Mountains in Tennessee when I was about seven years old. I'd never had apple fritters before, but it was obvious that my parents were no strangers, as they hunted down one particular restaurant just to partake in the treat, served alongside apple butter for dipping.

Apple lovers seem to hold these little handheld delights in such high regard that their eyes glaze over when talking of them. I've had more readers than I can count ask me if I had an apple fritter recipe, and so I'm bringing you my very own recipe for them, one that my husband swears could bring about world peace if I would only play my cards right and keep the sides of apple butter coming.

Vegetable oil

2 cups self-rising flour

½ cup brown sugar

1 teaspoon ground cinnamon

1 cup milk

3 tablespoons butter, melted

2 large eggs

2 cups peeled and diced apples

Confectioners' sugar, for serving, optional

Apple butter, for serving, see page 125

In a large skillet, pour vegetable oil to a depth of ½ inch and place on medium heat while you prepare the batter.

In a large bowl, mix the flour, brown sugar, and cinnamon together, using a fork to break up any lumps. Add the milk, melted butter, and eggs. Stir well to combine. Peel and dice the apples, add them to the batter, and stir. Drop by ⅛-cup measures into the hot oil and turn to brown on both sides. Drain on a paper towel–lined plate. Dust with confectioners' sugar, if desired. Serve with apple butter.

2 dozen

boiled peanuts

the first time I ever had boiled peanuts was when I was a girl, not more than seven or eight. My family and I took the first of many trips to the Smoky Mountains with one set of grandparents, Papa Reed and Cornetha. We were driving up the winding mountain roads when Cornetha saw a roadside vendor and wanted to stop. I couldn't figure out what had gotten her so excited, and when she bought a cup of wet peanuts, my curiosity was piqued. The peanuts had steam coming from them and the most delicious smell that set my stomach to grumbling. Cornetha ended up having a lot of help in eating that cupful of peanuts!

In the fall around the North Georgia mountains, you can always find a boiled peanut vendor set up at roadside stands or selling out of the back of their truck. I try to strategically plan a family trip to visit my husband's family this time of year just so I can enjoy this seasonal treat. There's nothing like being able to pull over and trade a couple of bills for a steaming cup of Georgia's finest. For those of you who don't want to marry a Georgian (or who may not have single Georgians readily available), here is how you can have this Southern delicacy in the comfort of your own home—while still maintaining a relationship with your non-Georgian spouse.

1 pound raw or green peanuts in the shell

1 cup salt

Place the peanuts in a large saucepan, cover with water, and add the salt. Bring to a boil, then reduce the heat and simmer for about 3 hours, adding more water if needed to keep them covered as they cook, until the peanuts are the tenderness and texture of a cooked bean. Place the entire peanut in your mouth to eat and then crack open with your teeth, drinking the juice and eating the peanut while discarding the shell.

2 to 3 servings

A Little History of Boiled Peanuts

Boiled peanuts have been popular in the South since at least the Civil War, when our troops used to carry them as part of their rations. With salt acting as a natural preservative, these boiled peanuts could be carried and eaten for up to a week, providing a quick nutritional source on the go and helping to make up for the lack of meat in the Southern soldier's diet.

melt-in-your-mouth doughnuts

don't let the fact that these doughnuts begin as canned biscuits fool ya—the end product is mouthwatering good and one of the best doughnuts I've ever had when served warm.

Tip: Mama says you should always drink a Diet Coke when eating doughnuts because it cancels out the calories.

Vegetable oil for frying

½ cup (1 stick) margarine, melted

1½ tablespoons ground cinnamon

1 cup sugar

One 10-count can Texas-style biscuits (or your preference, just not flaky layers)

Pour oil into a skillet to the depth of ½ inch and heat over medium to medium-high heat for about 5 minutes.

Place the margarine in a bowl. In a separate bowl, combine the cinnamon and sugar.

Using a plastic bottle cap, cut the center out of each biscuit. Lower the heat under the oil to medium. Drop the dough into the hot oil, watching carefully and turning when golden. Once the doughnuts are golden on both sides, remove to a paper towel–lined plate. Repeat until all the dough is cooked, including the doughnut holes.

Dip both sides of each doughnut into melted margarine, then press both sides into the cinnamon-sugar mixture. Serve warm.

10 doughnuts

the importance
of a doughnut shop

I was five years old when we took our first family vacation. My daddy had a brand-new truck, a 1979 silver Chevy Silverado, with a camper shell on back. He customized it with a special air horn that played "Dixieland" when you pressed this little black button under the dash, and we thought that was really something.

I remember so many details about that trip, it is hard to believe it was more than thirty years ago. What is funny is that I remember every single meal we ate out while we were gone, all three of them. You see, at home we didn't eat out. Mama always cooked every meal. Even on this trip we stayed at those little roadside hotels where you left a deposit and they gave you a bag of pots and pans to use. Mama brought groceries and a cooler.

We drove all night to get there, Mama and Daddy sitting in the front and my brother, sister, and me riding in the back of the truck, an air mattress squeezed in underneath us for comfort. It seemed like we stayed up all night, but it was likely only until ten or eleven. We laughed and told stories and my sister put all three of our inflatable swimming rings on and pretended she was a hula girl. It was so funny to us then that I still laugh now just thinking about it. My brother told us silly jokes, and the giddy excitement of the trip had everyone in fits until we finally fell asleep from exhaustion.

In the morning we took turns climbing through the window to the cab so Mama could get us all dressed, and after that was done we pulled over and stopped at a gas station for breakfast. Daddy let us pick out a snack cake, any one we wanted. It was the first time I had ever had raspberry snack cakes, and I got two of them in my package. To this day I think that was the most delicious breakfast I've ever eaten.

Another morning during that trip we ate at a restaurant that put a smiley face on your pancake with whipped cream—cherries for eyes and a sprinkled trail of chocolate chips for the mouth. I swear I remember every bite of that pancake.

We drove on to Daytona so we could see the ocean for the first time. I had a lime green swimsuit with a big yellow flower on the front. My head hurt when Mama made my ponytails that morning because I already had a red stripe sunburned into my part. I hardly slept the night before. It had been dark when we arrived, but I could hear the ocean so loud outside the window. I kept trying to imagine how it made so much noise.

I was so proud to be playing in the waves as I danced in and out of the receding waters and staked my claim on the biggest sandbox I had ever seen.

To adults, trips seem to pass by so quickly it feels you are arriving back home the day after you left. As a child, though, that trip seemed to go on forever, each day filled with new wonders and excitement. On the long drive home, Daddy pulled into a doughnut shop for breakfast. It was a national chain, and I'd never been to one before because we didn't have them in Alabama. We went in and our eyes were met with cases and cases of brightly iced doughnuts, flavors and sprinkles of all kinds. He let us pick out whichever one we wanted and I got one with pink icing and rainbow sprinkles. I have no idea what my brother or sister or anyone else got, I was far too enthralled with my prize.

The icing even tasted like strawberries.

We still don't have this doughnut chain where I live now, but I spotted one recently while on a weekend trip with my family. I told my husband I wanted to stop there on the way home and let the kids go in, even though we'd already had breakfast. We weren't going because we were hungry for food, anyway, I just wanted to share this experience with my own kids.

As we pulled in, I started telling them the story about how I ate there when I was a little girl and why it was so special because we didn't usually get to go to a doughnut shop, we didn't have money for things like that. Katy looked as if she heard "Blah blah blah doughnut, blah blah blah," and Brady looked at me as if to say, "It's a doughnut, Ma, get a grip."

They have no idea what it is like for a simple trip to a doughnut shop to be so special that you remember the colors of the sprinkles and the flavor of the icing three decades later.

They're used to chicken nugget kids meals, pantries filled to the brim, brand-name shoes, and $40 video games. They haven't a clue what it's like to be handed a pink iced doughnut and feel as if you've been given a tiara, magic wand, and pixie dust all at once.

So there I was, walking my kids into a doughnut shop and feeling gratitude for everything my parents have ever done for us. For how hard they worked and for how insistent they were on us doing well in school. For my dad holding down three jobs so Mama could stay home and look after us rather than having to leave us in day care or with a sitter. For them being at every school event we ever had and making it a point to brag on each report card we brought home.

I looked at the case and there they were, pink iced doughnuts with rainbow sprinkles, and for the first time I understood how much it must have meant to them to be able to give us such a treat that day. As my daughter glanced through the case and made her selection, I had to step away a moment when she chose the one with pink icing and rainbow sprinkles. I was in my mother's shoes at that moment, and Katy Rose was me right down to the two blond ponytails.

Thanks to the sacrifices of my parents, my kids will never know what it was like for a doughnut to be the highlight of a weeklong trip.

And I'm pretty grateful for that, too.

mexican cornbread

my mother makes the most delicious Mexican cornbread. It's moist and has just the right amount of spice. You can turn up the heat a little by adding extra jalapeños. I love to eat it hot, slathered with butter. Note: This batter is thinner than regular cornbread.

1½ **cups self-rising cornmeal**

1½ **tablespoons sugar**

½ **teaspoon salt**

¾ **cup shredded cheddar cheese**

½ **cup vegetable oil**

½ **cup chopped onion**

1 **jalapeño pepper, seeded and chopped**

¾ **cup milk**

1 **egg**

½ **cup canned cream-style corn**

Place a seasoned iron skillet in the oven and preheat to 350°F.

In a large bowl, mix all the ingredients together. Pour 1 tablespoon oil in the skillet and tilt to cover the bottom. Pour the batter in the skillet and bake for 30 to 40 minutes, until browned on top. Turn out onto a plate, cut, and serve.

8 servings

apple orchard snack cake

we have a tradition each year that has held since I was old enough to remember. My entire family piles into the car and we drive to Toney, Alabama, to visit our favorite orchard. As a child, I remember riding home in the back of the truck, munching on all varieties of fresh apples, and trying to guess what Mama would bake first with our bounty.

We would buy several baskets of different varieties, and once we got home, my mother would get to cooking. Each day, it seemed, there was a new apple dish waiting for us when we came in from school. We relished each and every one.

I often find with recipes, as with memories, it is the simple things that satisfy us the most. This recipe is the perfect example of that. A classic snack cake that is not too sweet, the simple ingredients make it a breeze to throw together. Add in the full flavor of locally grown apples (preferably from a family orchard trip!) and you can't go wrong. It is perfect for breakfast, with a cup of coffee while visiting friends, or any other time of day.

1 cup granulated sugar

½ cup (1 stick) butter or margarine, melted

3 eggs

2 cups graham cracker crumbs

2 to 3 apples, peeled, cored, and diced

¾ cup chopped walnuts, optional

Confectioners' sugar for sprinkling

Preheat the oven to 350°F and grease an 8 x 8-inch pan. Blend the granulated sugar, margarine, and eggs in a large bowl with a spoon. Stir in the graham cracker crumbs, apples, and walnuts until blended.

Spread the batter in the pan and bake for 40 to 45 minutes, until firm to the touch. Sprinkle liberally with confectioners' sugar. Cool and then cut into squares.

6 servings

apple spice muffins

I have never known anyone who did not absolutely love these muffins. One of the many great things about them, and what my mother liked so much with a large family to feed, is that you can use any type of apple and it makes no difference—they will still be just as good. You can also use apples that are starting to get a little soft and running out of their shelf life.

I try to make two batches so we have them to snack on for a few days afterward. This is my traditional "first day of school dish" that I take to welcome my children's teachers back from their summer vacation.

1¼ **cups self-rising flour (see Note)**

¾ **cup sugar**

½ **cup chopped nuts**

¼ **cup quick-cooking oats**

¾ **teaspoon ground cinnamon**

½ **teaspoon ground nutmeg**

2 **eggs**

2 **cups peeled, cored, and chopped apples**

¾ **cup vegetable oil**

1½ **tablespoons water**

Preheat the oven to 400°F and prepare a 12-hole muffin pan by spraying with cooking spray.

In a large bowl, mix together the flour, sugar, nuts, oats, cinnamon, and nutmeg.

In a separate bowl, beat the eggs and add the apples, oil, and water. Pour the egg mixture all at once into the flour mixture: stir just until the flour is moistened. Spoon the batter into muffin cups and bake for 20 minutes, or until lightly browned.

Note: If self-rising flour is unavailable, use all-purpose flour and add 1½ teaspoons baking powder and ½ teaspoon salt.

12 muffins

banana bread

leave it to Southerners to find a way to make rotting fruit into something delicious. Admittedly, "ripe" bananas aren't exactly rotten, but if you've seen the state of some bananas that have been behind this moist and delicious creation, you'd know what I mean.

I honestly don't know anyone who doesn't make banana bread on a regular basis. We see bananas going bad on our counter and our hands are already reaching for the flour. I'm certain this is another example to support my theory that all of the best Southern dishes came about out of necessity, when times were hard and starvation was a very real possibility.

This is my mother's recipe for banana bread and the one I grew up on. It's cakelike and absolutely delicious. Leftover slices are great toasted under the broiler and slathered with butter for breakfast. I often leave nuts out when baking to save money.

3 **bananas, peeled**

2 **cups sugar**

½ **cup (1 stick) margarine, softened**

1 **cup milk**

1 **cup chopped nuts, optional**

3 **cups self-rising flour**

2 **eggs**

1 **teaspoon vanilla extract**

Preheat the oven to 350°F and grease and flour two 8 x 4-inch loaf pans. Place the bananas in a large bowl and add the sugar. Mix until the bananas are liquefied. Add the margarine and mix until creamed together with the banana mixture. Add the remaining ingredients and blend well.

Pour into the loaf pans and bake for 1 hour, or until a toothpick inserted in the center comes out clean.

2 loaves

banana pecan french toast

if you'd like to pull out all the stops on an impressive breakfast, this is a must-have on the menu. Mama used to make it to surprise me on mornings when I had a special day ahead. Even now, I never tell my kids when I'm going to make it, instead opting to get up early and sneak into the kitchen so they can wake up to this special warm treat!

½ **cup half-and-half or milk**

4 **eggs, lightly beaten**

Pinch of salt

¼ **cup confectioners' sugar, plus more for serving, optional**

1 **teaspoon vanilla extract**

6 **thick slices egg or potato bread**

2 **bananas, sliced**

1 **cup chopped pecans**

Oil for cooking

Maple syrup, for serving

In a large, shallow bowl, mix the half-and-half, eggs, salt, confectioners' sugar, and vanilla together well. Dip only one side of one piece of bread into the batter. Place the dipped slice, batter side down, on wax paper. Layer banana slices on top of the bread. Dip a second slice of bread on both sides and put on top of the bananas (making a sandwich). Lay the sandwich on the chopped pecans and press slightly. Turn over onto additional chopped pecans and press again.

Brown on both sides in a medium-hot skillet in a small amount of oil. Sift additional confectioners' sugar over the top, if desired, before serving. Serve with maple syrup.

3 servings

there's magic
at the table

when I was a little girl, my mother got up early every morning to make a full breakfast for the five of us. While other kids went to school fueled by preservative-rich pastries and cold cereal, we started our day off with homemade biscuits, eggs, sausage gravy, and fresh fruit. These breakfasts were considered standard fare for us. We didn't think anything of it and neither did our mother, that's just how we were raised.

Her grandmother had done the same every day, sending ten kids off to school and work.

Just a short generation or two ago, meals were a time when family gathered together. They talked over their days, how hard they had worked, or what they expected to accomplish. Kids heard stories of their parents' youth and shared their latest dreams and schemes for life. In times past, the dinner table always served as the family's anchor, ensuring that no one person ever felt adrift. Granny, who was known for her wonderful cooking, knew that the true power of her flour and rolling pin was not in producing biscuits and tea cakes but in holding her children closer to her for a time, getting to know the tiny people within, and creating a family.

Today we seem to be growing more and more detached from one another. Sitting inches apart, kids are in their own world with handheld video games, MP3 players, and laptops. Parents may be sitting with the family, but their mind is on to-do lists and agendas, already mentally at work before having even left home.

For most people, expectations that seemed reasonable for our grandmothers are pretty much out of the question for us when it comes to preparing meals. Sometimes the only real time we gather together for a meal like our ancestors enjoyed is at family reunions or on the occasional Sunday.

Still, food seems to be a more popular topic now than ever before. Each month a new magazine and legion of books comes out alongside entire networks devoted to the topic. Despite the trend of celebrity chefs in the food world presenting us with fancy dishes with names most Southerners can't even pronounce, at the end of the day what we really want to come home to is the simple food we grew up on.

Though I consider myself to be a classic Southern cook, I'm also a modern one as well. In this day and age, with kids and schedules, not many of us have time to prepare a full breakfast each morning, and I have been known to take shortcuts to streamline school mornings on more than a few occasions.

But home cooks have always known how to slow down the pace of life.

Come any morning, as everyone bustles about preparing for their day, they will inevitably shuffle toward the kitchen with backpacks along their arms and computer bags in tow, and it's amazing the effect of seeing a home-cooked breakfast on the table has on everyone. There is a collective thud as belongings are quickly deposited and silence . . . actual silence as they all sit down and begin passing bowls around, smiling up at me between bites.

Next thing you know, we're talking. The din of electronic devices and clicking of phones dissipates into the words of my children, going over plans for their day or telling their latest silly joke—and in that moment, the world outside doesn't seem quite as pressing as it was only minutes before. Granny would be proud.

banana crumb cake

I love crumb cakes. Not too sweet, more filling than regular cake, and with that delicious crumbly topping, you just can't go wrong. In my eternal quest not to waste food, I came up with this recipe as a twist on our old banana bread as another way to use up almost-too-ripe bananas.

The reception from my family and friends as well as my Southern Plate family was amazing, and it's become a standard at our home and a recipe I'm always asked to share.

You can make this cake in a 9 x 13-inch pan if you like, but I like to split it up so I can give one away. If you make it in a 9 x 13-inch pan, just pour half of your batter in, top with half of the crumbs, then the remaining batter and remaining crumbs.

3 bananas, peeled

2 cups granulated sugar

½ cup (1 stick) margarine

1 cup milk

1 cup chopped nuts, optional

2 cups self-rising flour

2 eggs

1 teaspoon vanilla extract

Crumb Topping

½ cup (1 stick) margarine

1 cup brown sugar (dark or light)

1 cup flour (self-rising or all-purpose, whatever you have on hand)

Preheat the oven to 350°F and spray two 8 x 8-inch pans with cooking spray. Place the bananas in a large bowl and add the sugar. Mix until the bananas are liquefied. Add the margarine and mix until creamed together with the banana mixture. Add the remaining ingredients and blend well.

In a medium bowl, combine all the topping ingredients. Cut together with a long-tined fork until well blended. Pour one quarter of the batter into each pan and top with one quarter of the crumb mixture. Pour the remaining batter over and top with the remaining crumb mixture. Bake for 45 minutes to 1 hour, until a toothpick inserted in the center comes out clean. Serve from the pan.

12 servings

Cheap Vanilla

Most anyone who is in the know about cooking will tell you that the best vanilla is one that is pure, imported from Timbuktu, and costs a pretty penny. I'm all about having favorites, and I'm sure fancy vanilla is every bit as fancy as the price, but I still use good old imitation vanilla in everything I bake and seldom pay more than a dollar for a bottle of it. Haven't had a complaint yet!

homemade caramel corn

I don't know how Thanksgiving works with your family, but I imagine it is somewhat similar to how it works with mine. Siblings, spouses, kidders, grandmothers, aunts, uncles, and anyone else who happens to want a good meal that day gathers at my mother's house. Most of us come in toting various dishes and add them to the already heavily laden table of goodies. My mother's oven is still going full blast with rolls, mac and cheese, or perhaps even the turkey. The smell of pies, cinnamon, smoked meats, and yeast rolls is so good it is positively torturous. If you weren't hungry before, you sure are now!

Several years back, I got the bright idea of making homemade caramel corn to take to Thanksgiving in order to help fight off the munchies until dinnertime. Not only was it a hit with the kids (and kept them considerably more patient), but the adults seemed to delight in being able to grab a handful of something to snack on even more. This is now my personal Thanksgiving tradition—Aunt Christy brings the caramel corn.

1 cup (2 sticks) margarine

1 cup honey

1 cup packed brown sugar

1 teaspoon salt

½ teaspoon baking soda

1 teaspoon vanilla extract

1 teaspoon butter flavoring (or you can use more vanilla)

3 gallons popped popcorn

Preheat the oven to 250°F. Grease 2 large baking sheets.

In a heavy saucepan, combine the margarine, honey, brown sugar, and salt. Place over medium heat and stir continuously until the mixture comes to a boil. Stop stirring and let boil, undisturbed, for 3 minutes. Remove from the heat and stir in the baking soda, vanilla and, butter flavoring. Place half of the cooled popcorn in a large dishpan (I do mine in two batches) and pour half the caramel sauce over. Stir until evenly coated. Spread onto a baking sheet and repeat with the remainder on another baking sheet.

Place in the oven and bake for 1 hour, stirring every 15 minutes. Allow to cool and break apart, then store in an airtight container.

about 20 servings

chicken stew

this is a classic chicken stew that has been in my family for almost forty years. Mama got the recipe out of a magazine in the seventies, where it was submitted by a sweet-looking little old lady. Mama took one look at her photograph next to the recipe and said, "She just looks like she makes good food."

I've had many readers try this stew and say it was just like their grandmother's, but they'd never found a recipe able to duplicate it until this one. It is perfect for a gathering because it actually tastes better the second day. I like to make it a day ahead of time, store it in the refrigerator, and warm it on the stovetop right before my guests arrive. Leftovers (if there are any) freeze very well.

One 3- to 4-pound chicken

- 7 **cups water**
- 6 **medium potatoes, peeled and diced**
- 2 **cups frozen or canned whole kernel corn**
- 2 **large onions, chopped**
- 4 **cups canned tomatoes**
- 3 **tablespoons sugar**
- 5 **teaspoons salt**
- 2 **teaspoons black pepper**
- 2 **tablespoons butter**

Place the chicken in a large pot and cover with the water. Bring to a boil. Reduce the heat to medium and cook until tender, approximately 1 hour. Remove the chicken from the broth and remove the skin and the meat from the bones. Shred or tear the chicken into pieces. Dip off the excess fat that forms on top of the broth. Place the potatoes in a separate pot and pour enough broth over them to cover. Cover and simmer until just tender. Do not drain.

Mash the potatoes slightly, using a potato masher or fork, keeping them lumpy. To the original pot that you cooked the chicken in, add the corn, onions, tomatoes, sugar, salt, pepper, and the remainder of the broth. Cover and simmer for 20 minutes. Add the potatoes and chicken and simmer slowly with the lid off for 30 to 45 minutes. Just before serving, stir in the butter and let it melt. Serve hot.

12 servings

chocolate cobbler

growing up, I always thought the reason we had this so often was because everyone liked it so much, but according to Mama, the frequency of this dessert had a lot more to do with it being so quick, easy, and, most importantly, budget friendly. Generally, most folks have these ingredients on hand. It doesn't hurt that you don't even need an egg for it.

This cobbler bakes up magically. When you pull it out of the oven you'll have a rich chocolate cake layer on top and a hot fudge saucy layer beneath. I highly recommend serving it with ice cream.

We frequently package the dry ingredients and give them along with the recipe as Christmas gifts. See page 175 for instructions.

1 cup self-rising flour

¾ cup granulated sugar

¼ cup plus 2 tablespoons unsweetened cocoa powder

½ cup milk

1 teaspoon vanilla extract

2 tablespoons vegetable oil

1 cup chopped pecans, optional

¾ cup brown sugar

1¾ cups hot water

Preheat the oven to 350°F and grease an 8 x 8-inch baking pan.

In a large bowl, mix together the flour, granulated sugar, and 2 tablespoons of the cocoa powder. Add the milk, vanilla, oil, and nuts, if using. Mix well. Pour into the baking pan.

In a small bowl, mix the brown sugar and ¼ cup cocoa powder together. Sprinkle over the batter. Very slowly pour the hot tap water over the dry mixture and batter. (Be sure you pour the water slowly or you'll mix up the ingredients. I put my water in a measuring cup and gently pour it into the dish over the batter.)

Bake for 40 to 45 minutes. To test for doneness, stick a toothpick in no more than ½ inch. If it comes out clean, the cobbler is done.

6 servings

terri's dixie cornbread

my dear friend Terri contacted me shortly after happening upon Southern Plate to tell me she had a world-famous cornbread recipe that used two whole cups of buttermilk and had been declared "better than Mama's" by her Southern-born husband. She asked if I'd like the recipe, and I jumped at the chance to be able to make a dish that had earned such lofty praise. Terri shared her recipe with me, and a friendship was born. I know you'll love it every bit as much as I do. I've never had cornbread so moist in all my born days.

1 tablespoon shortening

1½ cups enriched white cornmeal

3 tablespoons all-purpose flour

1 teaspoon salt

1 teaspoon baking soda

2 cups buttermilk (see Note)

1 egg

2 tablespoons bacon drippings or melted butter

Preheat the oven to 450°F. Place the shortening in a 10-inch cast-iron skillet, and preheat in the oven.

In a large bowl, sift together the dry ingredients; add the buttermilk, egg, and drippings, and mix just until the dry ingredients are moistened.

Pour into the greased hot skillet and bake for 20 to 25 minutes, until brown. Serve warm with butter.

Note: See page 265 for how to make your own buttermilk.

8 servings

christy's chili

any Southerner worth his salt has a great chili recipe, preferably a signature one. This is why I set out several years back trying out this one and that, tweaking and adding until I came up with one I could call my own.

This recipe has developed over the years, and most days I make it in the slow cooker so I don't have to fret over it or remember to stir throughout the day.

If you brown and freeze your meat ahead of time (like I do), this becomes a "toss it in and turn it on" type meal—a favorite for busy days. I like to keep my dishes on the mild side as far as spiciness goes because I usually feed wee ones, but you can amp this recipe up by adding in hot sauce or jalapeños while it's cooking.

2 pounds ground beef

One 29-ounce can kidney beans (with liquid)

One 29-ounce can pinto beans (with liquid)

One 29-ounce can tomato sauce

1 cup diced onion

½ cup diced green chiles

3 medium tomatoes or one 29-ounce can diced tomatoes

2 teaspoons salt

1½ teaspoons black pepper

2 cups water

3 tablespoons chili powder

¼ cup diced celery

2 teaspoons ground cumin

In a large skillet over medium-high heat, brown the ground beef until no longer pink and drain off the fat.

In a large pot or slow cooker, combine the beef with the remaining ingredients. If cooking in a pot, bring to a simmer over low heat and cook, stirring every 15 minutes, for 2 to 3 hours. If cooking in a slow cooker, stir to combine and cover. Cook on low for 7 to 8 hours or high for 3 to 4 hours.

8 servings

corn chowder

this corn chowder can easily be made vegetarian by substituting a vegetable broth for the chicken broth.

It is hearty, filling, oh-so-warm, and has just the right blend of flavors. I adore it. Special thanks to my sister-in-law, Tina Jordan, for passing this recipe on to me many years back.

2 tablespoons margarine

1 medium onion, chopped

1 medium green bell pepper, chopped

One 14.5-ounce can chicken broth

2 large red potatoes, cubed

1 jalapeño pepper, seeded and chopped

2 teaspoons Dijon mustard

1 teaspoon salt

½ teaspoon paprika

¼ to ½ teaspoon crushed red pepper flakes

3 cups frozen corn kernels

4 green onions, chopped

3 cups milk

½ cup all-purpose flour

In a large saucepan, melt the margarine over medium heat. Add the onion and bell pepper and sauté until tender. Add the broth and potatoes. Bring to a boil, then reduce the heat, cover, and simmer for 15 minutes. Stir in the jalapeño, mustard, salt, paprika, and red pepper flakes. Add the corn, green onions, and 2½ cups of the milk. Bring to a boil.

Meanwhile, back at the ranch, combine the flour and remaining ½ cup milk and mix well. Gradually add this mixture to the chowder and bring to a boil, stirring constantly, and cook for 2 minutes, or until thick and bubbly.

8 servings

chocolate pound cake

if you're looking for health food, this is the one to skip. But if you want a good old-fashioned pound cake unlike any other, head on into the kitchen with this recipe. I always top this with Grandma Pearl's Flaky Chocolate Icing (page 102), but you can leave it plain or put a dusting of confectioners' sugar over the top if you like.

1½ **cups (3 sticks) margarine or butter, softened**

3 **cups sugar**

5 **eggs**

3 **cups all-purpose flour**

½ **cup unsweetened cocoa powder**

½ **teaspoon baking powder**

1 **cup milk**

1 **tablespoon vanilla extract (yes, a whole tablespoon!)**

Grandma Pearl's Flaky Chocolate Icing (recipe follows)

Preheat the oven to 325°F. Grease and flour a Bundt pan.

Cream the margarine in a large bowl. Add the sugar and beat until light and fluffy. Add the eggs, one at a time, beating well after each addition.

In a separate bowl, whisk together the flour, cocoa powder, and baking powder. Measure the milk and stir the vanilla into it. Alternately add the milk and dry ingredients, mixing after each addition. Pour into the pan and bake for 1 hour and 20 minutes, or until a toothpick inserted in the center comes out clean. Let cool for 10 minutes before removing from the pan and cool completely before icing.

12 servings

grandma pearl's
flaky chocolate icing

this is what the old folks refer to as a "boiled icing." This means they make it in a pot on top of the oven and it is brought to a boil until it thickens. It is very much like making fudge, but we use a timer instead of a thermometer to trust it gets to the right temperature.

Have you ever had your granny make one of those cakes that when she cuts into it, the icing cracks and breaks off in huge fudgy chunks? This is that icing. This icing hardens very quickly, so it's easiest to use on a sheet cake, where you simply pour it over the cake while it's still in the pan and allow it to cool. If you'd like the peanut butter version of this icing, it can be found on page 258.

1½ **cups sugar**

½ **cup unsweetened cocoa powder**

7 **tablespoons milk (see Note)**

2 **tablespoons shortening**

2 **tablespoons margarine**

¼ **teaspoon salt**

1 **teaspoon vanilla extract**

Combine the sugar, cocoa powder, milk, shortening, margarine, and salt in a heavy saucepan. Bring to a rolling boil, stirring constantly. Once it reaches a boil, allow to boil without stirring for 2 minutes, or until it reaches the soft-ball stage. Remove from the heat and add the vanilla. Stir until just slightly cooled. Pour over the cooled cake.

Note: I know you're going to be tempted not to measure out the milk, but you're going to have to. Eyeballing it will mess up this icing every time. I know from experience!

enough to frost two 9-inch layers or one 9 x 13-inch sheet cake

money can just as easily buy misery as it can happiness

years ago, when my son was a toddler, my husband got a job offer. We loved the company he was with, as they were very family-oriented and offered lots of opportunities for growth and advancement, but the amount of money offered to us by the new job as a young family was something we felt we didn't have the right to refuse.

I'll never forget the conversation we had about it—both of us sat looking at each other like we'd just found out someone had died, talking about how we were going to be making so much more money and all of the opportunities that would bring financially. There was no joy, only dread and a feeling that we didn't have a choice because of the dollar signs involved.

With heavy hearts, we made the move.

I don't know why folks don't trust their intuition more. That inner voice will keep you out of more trouble than anything in this world, and we've learned through the years to trust in ourselves when it comes to that feeling of dread, thankfully through what I consider gentler lessons. Good situations should bring about good feelings—if they bring about dread and foreboding, then something is wrong.

We relocated near Atlanta, into Granny Jordan's house. Granny had recently passed away but had offered her house to us just before she passed when she heard of the job. We planned on it being only temporary, a way to settle in to the new area a bit and also spend a little time mourning the loss of such a wonderful woman.

For three months we lived in Granny Jordan's house, and for three months we were pretty much miserable and missing our old home terribly. Although we had a wonderful chance to be close to Ricky's family, his new job had him traveling constantly, home mostly on weekends. That was just enough time to get his laundry done and cook a few meals before he was off again. We missed our old company and its family values that had Dad home by dinnertime and traveling only once in a blue moon.

There was a plus side to this, though, as there is to every situation. While staying in Granny Jordan's house, I learned something about her that I'd never known before: She was an avid collector of recipes. In her back room, I found card file after card file filled to the brim with recipes written in her hand, given to her by friends, or clipped out of newspapers and magazines. She'd carefully written on each one when she'd prepared it, her thoughts on the end product, and who she'd served it to along with dates.

Realizing what a treasure I'd found, I set out to type up all of the recipes in one document. I set up my computer on the screened-in porch overlooking Lake Lanier and typed away all during the day, especially during Brady's naptime. I spent the better part of three months doing this, and one day Ricky and I decided that we needed to move back to our home. He talked to his new company, and they agreed to let him work from Alabama and travel, using our original home as his base. When we moved back, I took the unfinished card files with me to complete and return later. I spent the better part of a year cataloguing Granny Jordan's recipes and then added in every single recipe from my family as well. I called all of my grandmothers, borrowed Mama's handwritten book, tracked down aunts, and even stood over my own granny's shoulder a time or two to personally measure out the recipes that she just "kept in her head" in order to preserve these for all of us. By the time Christmas rolled around, I had a book of more than five hundred recipes, and I have drawn mostly from that book for SouthernPlate.com as well as this book.

Meanwhile, Ricky continued to travel. Brady missed his daddy and I missed having a husband beyond weekend laundry dropoffs. We made the decision to try to get "our" old job back, even if it meant a pay cut. Shortly after he inquired, they welcomed him back, completely reinstating him as if he'd never left. Now that's what I mean by a gentle lesson!

We were able to learn, firsthand, that money is not nearly as important as it seems and that money can just as easily provide misery as it can happiness. We were able to learn the value of working for an employer who has the same value system that we do, and in the process of learning that lesson I was able to uncover and develop a treasure that will be cherished by my family, and hopefully yours, for generations to come.

Since then we've had a few people and companies flash dollar signs before both of our eyes for one reason or another, but we're able to see right through them to what matters most. Money is a shallow thing when you think of all of the things that it can't buy. That's where the real wealth lies.

fried apples

most years on our birthday we get to pick a special meal for Mama to prepare for us. I always go for a full country breakfast, served at suppertime. Homemade biscuits, country ham, hash brown casserole, scrambled eggs, bacon, and these special fried apples.

Of course, no one person can actually manage to eat even a portion of everything prepared, but it sure does lay out for a grand-looking meal!

2½ cups apple juice

4 large Golden Delicious apples, unpeeled and cut into wedges

¼ cup sugar

3 tablespoons cornstarch

1 teaspoon ground cinnamon

¼ teaspoon ground allspice

In a large skillet, combine the apple juice and sliced apples. Place over medium heat and cook until the apples are fork-tender, turning often for even cooking. Be careful not to overcook the apples. Remove the apples from the juice with a slotted spoon and place in a large bowl.

In another bowl, combine the remaining ingredients and stir with a wire whisk until well blended. Pour the hot apple juice into the dry mixture. Whisk vigorously until the lumps are gone. Pour this mixture back into the skillet and heat over medium heat, whisking constantly, until bubbly and thick. Remove from the heat and pour over the apples in the bowl. Stir until the apples are evenly coated.

6 servings

good 'n easy apple cake

serve this cake warm, with homemade whipped cream over the top, and you're in for a treat unlike any you've ever known! I really enjoy it because it isn't too sweet. I'm not a big icing person, but give me fresh whipped cream oozing down over warm cake and you've got one happy camper on your hands.

This recipe came from a friend of my mother's, Mrs. Hiles. We met her when I was eight years old, and she had the first non-Southern accent I had ever heard. She was from Pennsylvania, and I just loved to hear her talk. She was good-hearted and kind to all, especially children. I always think of her whenever I make this cake.

One 21-ounce can apple pie filling
1 box white cake mix
3 eggs
1 cup chopped nuts

topping
½ cup all-purpose flour
½ cup sugar
1 teaspoon ground cinnamon
1 cup chopped pecans
4 tablespoons (½ stick) margarine or butter, softened

Preheat the oven to 350°F and grease a 9 x 13-inch baking pan. Pour the apple pie filling out onto a large plate and coarsely chop it up with a knife. Place it in a large bowl and add all the other ingredients; mix well. Pour into the baking pan.

Mix all the topping ingredients well with a fork and sprinkle over the top of the cake.

Bake the cake for 50 to 55 minutes, or until a toothpick inserted in the center comes out clean. Serve warm with homemade whipped cream on top (or store-bought if you prefer).

12 servings

steak and milk gravy

this is one of my absolute favorite meals that my mother made while I was growing up. Tender steak smothered in creamy and flavorful milk gravy. This dish is yet another bit of proof that simple food is oftentimes the best.

Back in the day, grocery stores didn't have cubed steak. My great-grandmother would buy round steak and use the side of a saucer to beat the meat in order to tenderize it, until it looked like cubed steak does today. My mother said it was the most delicious thing she had ever tasted. I know, though, that my saucers are thankful we can get cubed steak at the market these days.

I always seem to have luck finding packages of cubed steak on sale. I divide them up into individual bags and freeze them to make a quick lunch of steak and milk gravy from time to time. I don't like going to the trouble of cooking just for me, so it's always a treat when I do.

Vegetable oil

1¼ **cups all-purpose flour**

¼ **teaspoon salt, plus more for the gravy**

¼ **teaspoon pepper, plus more for the gravy**

4 **pieces cubed steak, approximately 4 ounces each**

1½ **cups milk**

Place enough oil in a pan to just coat the bottom, and place over medium heat while you prepare your steak.

In a shallow bowl, combine 1 cup of the flour with the salt and pepper. Stir that up. Dip each piece of steak into flour on both sides to get it coated well. Place each piece of steak in the pan and cook until good and browned on both sides. Remove the steak to a plate while you make your gravy.

Place the remaining ¼ cup flour into the skillet with the meat drippings. Add a little more salt and pepper and stir over medium heat until the flour is lightly browned (just a few minutes). Slowly pour in the milk, stirring constantly. Reduce the heat to low and continue stirring with a wire whisk to break up any lumps, until thickened and there are no lumps. This will happen rather quickly. Add a little more milk if you prefer thinner gravy. Return the steak to the pan and turn to coat with gravy on both sides.

Serve the steak and gravy together in a bowl or serve the gravy on the side to go with mashed potatoes.

4 servings

mama's meatloaf

the only thing more comforting than meatloaf is leftover meatloaf, heated and served up between two slices of bread, sandwich style. Sometimes my mama makes extra just so she can have enough for sandwiches the next day. This is my mama's meatloaf recipe, one that she swears by. I hope you enjoy it as much as we have over the years.

2 **pounds ground chuck**

One **8-ounce can tomato sauce**

½ **cup cracker crumbs or quick-cooking oats**

2 **eggs, beaten**

½ **cup chopped onion**

⅓ **cup chopped bell pepper**

1 **clove garlic, diced**

1 **teaspoon salt**

½ **teaspoon black pepper**

2 to 3 **tablespoons ketchup**

Preheat the oven to 400°F. In a large bowl, mix all the ingredients except the ketchup together well. Form into a loaf, pressing firmly to compact the loaf (this helps seal in the juices).

Place in a loaf pan and bake for 1 hour. Remove from the oven and spread the ketchup over the top. Put back in the oven for 10 minutes more. Pour the grease off the meatloaf and let rest for 10 minutes before serving.

8 servings

granny jordan's apple skillet cake

this cake is positively infused with flavor. The texture is ultra-tender and moist. Visually, it is every bit as appealing as it tastes. Apples glazed with butter and sugar are arranged over the top with a generous sprinkling of pecans, and when cut, the interior of the cake is speckled generously with cinnamon. It's unlike anything you've ever tasted or could hope to find in a restaurant. No matter how many times I make it, my family and guests always react with awe.

⅓ cup margarine

1 cup sugar

1¼ teaspoons ground cinnamon

5 to 6 apples, peeled and sliced

½ cup pecans

1 cup self-rising flour

3 tablespoons margarine, melted

1 egg, well beaten

⅓ cup evaporated milk

⅓ cup water

Melt ⅓ cup margarine in a large skillet over medium heat. Stir in ⅔ cup of the sugar and 1 teaspoon of the cinnamon. Top with the apple slices; cover and cook for 10 minutes. Top with the pecans.

In a medium bowl, stir together the flour, the remaining ⅓ cup sugar, and remaining ¾ teaspoon cinnamon. Combine the 3 tablespoons melted margarine, the egg, milk, and water in a separate bowl. Add to the flour mixture and mix until just moistened. Spoon over the hot apples and pecans. Reduce the heat to low, cover, and cook for 20 minutes, or until firm to the touch. Turn out onto a large plate to serve.

8 servings

hamburger stew

of the many things busy families have in common, one common factor I've always found is a love for ground beef. We ate far more than our share growing up because of the affordability and versatility of this meat. Nowadays I purchase my ground beef in large quantities and cook it up all at once, then drain off the grease and divide it up into small bags to freeze for streamlined meals.

You won't find a lot of spices or seasonings in this recipe because I rely on the spicy vegetable juice to produce a fully-bodied flavor. Don't worry, though, the end result is not spicy and very kid-friendly. In fact, I have to make extra because my son seems to always come back with an empty bowl. It can be assembled in the morning and put in your slow cooker all day on low. If making it this way, just go ahead and add the ground beef at the start. I add it in last to keep it a little firmer. Instant mashed potato flakes serve as an excellent thickener if you'd like a little more body to your stew. Stir in 2 tablespoons and then add more to suit your personal taste.

This recipe is a great starting point. Play with ingredients and make it your own!

4 carrots, diced

1 onion, chopped

5 to 6 potatoes, peeled and diced

2 cups frozen green beans

One 29-ounce can diced or crushed tomatoes

1 to 2 cans spicy hot V-8 juice (I use 2)

2 cups water

4 beef bouillon cubes

1 teaspoon salt, or to taste

1 to 2 pounds ground beef, cooked and drained

Place everything in a pot except for the ground beef. Bring to a boil over medium-high heat, then reduce the heat to a simmer. Cover and cook for 1 hour, or until the vegetables are tender. Add the ground beef and cook for another 30 minutes.

8 servings

crunchy beef casserole

this casserole was one of the recipes I discovered during the brief time we lived at Granny Jordan's house. It was written in her own hand on a faded old index card. It's filling, economical, and comfort food at its finest. I don't know about you, but I can always use another good ground beef recipe.

2 cups corkscrew macaroni (rotini)

1 pound ground beef

One 10.5-ounce can cream of mushroom soup

¾ cup shredded cheddar cheese

¾ teaspoon seasoned salt

One 14-ounce can diced tomatoes

¾ cup chopped green pepper, optional (I leave it out for the kids)

1 can french-fried onions

Preheat the oven to 350°F and grease a 2-quart casserole dish.

Cook the macaroni as directed on the package; rinse and drain.

Brown the beef in a large skillet over medium-high heat until no longer pink. Drain the fat. Combine all the ingredients except the french-fried onions in the casserole dish. Cover and bake for 30 minutes, then uncover, top with the french-fried onions, and bake for 5 minutes longer.

8 servings

please
share your recipes

it comes as little surprise to anyone that I always share my recipes. I've been adamant about this since day one; I consider it an honor when I am asked to share a recipe.

I often receive e-mails from readers, though, telling me about beloved dishes of those who have passed away that they could never duplicate because the recipe either wasn't written down or was kept secret. One such e-mail that really tore at my heart I received right after I posted the recipe for my Granny Lela's fried peach pies:

> *My great-grandmother always made fried peach pies. We loved her so much, and she passed away two years ago. We've missed her terribly and no one has ever been able to duplicate her pies. I tried your recipe and they were just like hers. It was just like Granny was with us again.*

These kinds of letters really make my heart ache because I know exactly what the writer is saying. It's not so much about the recipes as it is the person who made them. Being able to recreate that recipe in memory of her dear granny brought her back in a tangible way. Even now I can't make one of Lela's recipes without imagining her sitting beside me, her hands clasped over her faded cotton dress as she smiles in contentment.

This is one of the greatest motivations for me in writing about Southern foods, to preserve our most cherished recipes from our most cherished family members. In today's world of online communities devoted to newfangled foods and eclectic styles of eating, the old ways, the simple ways, seem to be cast aside. Meanwhile, new generations are leaving us behind, and with them, our history.

When I ask for a recipe, it's not so I can steal your thunder in the kitchen. It's so I can bring a little bit of your heart into mine.

So, please, share your recipes. If you love someone enough to cook for them, please write down the recipe so that they can feel your love still, even after you're no longer there to give it.

lela's fried fruit pies

these are my great-grandmother's pies. I remember Lela standing in the kitchen humming as she fried these, placing the crispy treats on a paper towel–lined plate next to the stove as she dipped more into the hot oil in her cast-iron skillet. The entire house smelled of peaches, because that was her favorite kind of fruit pie.

If you're yearning for an old-fashioned fried pie like Granny used to make, you've come to the right place. This recipe can easily be modified to accommodate your favorite dried fruit. Feel free to modify it to accommodate your own tastes. Most folks start out making these with dried apples but even though we love apples, nothing can beat a fried pie made with dried peaches.

filling

- 6 to 7 ounces dried fruit (I used peaches; you can also use apples, apricots, or other dried fruit)
- 2 cups water
- 1 cup sugar
- 4 tablespoons (½ stick) butter or margarine
- 1 tablespoon lemon juice
- ½ teaspoon ground cinnamon

Place the dried fruit in a large saucepan and add the water and sugar. Bring to a boil over medium-high heat, then reduce the heat to a simmer and cook until the fruit is tender and the sugar is dissolved, about 20 minutes. Add all the other ingredients and mash together with a potato masher or fork. Set aside while you prepare the dough.

dough

- 2 cups all-purpose flour
- 1 teaspoon salt
- ½ cup shortening
- ½ cup milk, plus more if needed
- Vegetable oil

To make the dough, in a medium bowl, combine the flour and salt. Cut in the shortening with a long-tined fork. Add the milk and stir until the dough sticks together. Divide into 10 portions. Roll each portion out on a floured surface into a 5- or 6-inch circle. Place 2 tablespoons of filling in each. Wet the edges and fold over, crimping with a fork.

In a large skillet, pour the oil to a depth of ¼ inch and heat over medium heat. Add the fruit pies to the hot oil and fry until browned on both sides, 3 to 4 minutes, turning as needed. Remove to a paper towel–lined plate.

10 pies

aunt sue's chocolate fried pies

in the South, families tend to spread out and adopt other members into them. While Aunt Sue isn't officially related by blood, she and her husband (Uncle Jerry) have been around as long as I can remember, and so you could say we just annexed them into the family. Once you try her fried chocolate pies, you just might be calling her Aunt Sue, too!

filling

- **2 cups sugar**
- **6 tablespoons unsweetened cocoa powder**
- **½ cup (1 stick) butter or margarine, melted**

In a medium bowl, stir together the sugar and cocoa powder. Add the melted butter and stir until the mixture forms a paste. Set aside while you prepare the dough.

dough

- **2 cups all-purpose flour**
- **1 teaspoon salt**
- **½ cup shortening**
- **½ cup milk, plus more if needed**
- **Vegetable oil**

In a medium bowl, combine the flour and salt. Cut in the shortening with a long-tined fork. Add the milk and stir until the dough sticks together. Divide into 10 portions. Roll each portion out on a floured surface into a 5- or 6-inch circle. Place 2 tablespoons of filling in each. Wet the edges and fold over, crimping with a fork.

In a large skillet, pour the oil to a depth of ¼ inch and heat over medium heat. Place the chocolate pies in the hot oil and fry until browned on both sides, turning as needed. Remove to a paper towel–lined plate.

10 pies

lucy's sweet potato casserole

this is my grandmother Lucille's special sweet potato casserole that always gets rave reviews whenever we take it anywhere. Mama recently ate in a fancy restaurant in Nashville and was told that she simply had to try the sweet potato casserole. She ordered it, took one bite, and declared that it was exactly like Grandmama's. Despite the sweetness, we like to serve this as a side dish. Technically, sweet potatoes are a vegetable, so it works!

2 to 3 large sweet potatoes (to make 3 cups cooked)

½ cup (1 stick) margarine

2 eggs

1 cup granulated sugar

1 teaspoon vanilla extract

1 teaspoon ground cinnamon

One 3.5-ounce can sweetened flaked coconut

topping

1 cup all-purpose flour

1 cup brown sugar

½ cup (1 stick) margarine

1 cup chopped pecans

Preheat the oven to 350°F.

Peel and slice the sweet potatoes. Place in a large saucepan and cover with water. Bring to a boil, then reduce the heat and cook until fork-tender, 30 to 45 minutes. Drain well and place in a large bowl.

Add the margarine and beat with an electric mixer until smooth. Add the eggs, one at a time, while the mixer is going. Add the sugar, vanilla, and cinnamon, and mix well. Toss in the coconut and blend. Spread onto a pie plate and bake for 20 minutes.

While the casserole is in the oven, make the topping. In a large bowl, stir together the flour and brown sugar, breaking up any lumps. Cut in the margarine and stir in the pecans. Spoon or sprinkle on top of the sweet potato mixture. Return to the oven and continue baking until golden and bubbly, about 20 minutes more.

8 servings

mama reed's apple dapple cake

don't you just love the taste of brown sugar? I mean, all on its own, I just love brown sugar. Whenever I am baking with it, I can't help but get a pinch out for myself. Lucky is the day when I find a few precious lumps within the bag.

The wonderful thing about this cake (and Lord, I do mean *wonderful*) is that the resulting flavor is a perfect blend of fresh apples and buttery brown sugar. With the special sauce poured over the cake and allowed to soak in before removing the cake from the pan, it is by far the moistest cake I've ever baked. As if the flavor (and smell!) were not enough, the slices are gorgeous, too. Thick slices showcase bits of apple and the slightly granular texture around the edges of the tender crust brought on by the brown sugar. If you've ever wanted to win someone over through their stomach, this cake is a home run. It may not be a good idea to be left alone with this cake. Personally, I could never trust myself. It just tastes too good, and I swear it whispers my name. Christy . . . Christy . . .

Mama always uses a tube pan when baking this cake, as well as her vanilla wafer cake (page 11), but I don't like to fuss with tube pans, so I always use a Bundt pan.

cake

- 1 cup vegetable oil
- 2 cups granulated sugar
- 3 eggs
- 2 teaspoons vanilla extract
- 3 cups all-purpose flour
- 1 teaspoon salt
- 1 teaspoon baking soda
- 1 chopped pecans
- 3 cups peeled and finely chopped apples

Preheat the oven to 350°F and grease and flour a tube or Bundt pan.

In a large bowl, mix together the oil, sugar, eggs, and vanilla.

In a separate bowl, sift together the flour, salt, and baking soda. Add to the wet mixture. Fold in the pecans and apples. Bake for 1 hour.

sauce

- 1 cup packed brown sugar
- ¼ cup milk
- ¾ cup margarine

While the cake is in the oven, make the sauce: In a medium saucepan, combine the brown sugar, milk, and margarine. Place over medium heat and bring to a gentle boil. Cook for 3 minutes, stirring constantly to dissolve the sugar. Pour over the hot cake while the cake is still in the pan. Let the sauce soak in and the cake cool completely before removing it from the pan.

12 servings

my special apple pie

don't you just hate it when you taste something positively divine that a friend made, ask for the recipe, and they refuse to give it to you? How awkward is that? I have made it a point to share any and every recipe that has ever been requested of me. I have to admit, though, that this one has tempted me to stray from that policy. So I am going to include it here in an effort to remain true to my own creed.

This recipe is actually quite easy. The most difficult and time-consuming part is simply peeling and "chipping" or thinly slicing the apples. I like to cut mine in chips rather than slices because they stack up better and make for a neater and prettier pie. Don't say you got this recipe out of a cookbook or make any other excuses. When (not if, but when) someone tells you how divine your pie is, I want you to smile graciously and say "thank you." This is now *your* apple pie recipe.

My father-in-law, Rick, is an apple pie aficionado. Imagine how honored I was when he declared my apple pie to be the best he'd ever tasted—just like his Granny White's did.

1 package refrigerated pie crusts (2 crusts)

9 or 10 apples (use a combination of Granny Smith and one other variety)

¾ cup sugar

¼ cup cornstarch

1 teaspoon ground cinnamon

½ teaspoon ground allspice

Dash of salt

¼ cup apple juice

2 tablespoons lemon juice

Preheat the oven to 425°F. Roll one pie crust out into a pie plate. Peel and chip the apples into a large bowl.

In a separate bowl, combine the sugar, cornstarch, cinnamon, allspice, and salt and stir to blend. Combine the apple juice and lemon juice in another bowl and stir to blend. Pour the dry and wet ingredients over the apples and stir well.

Place 1 pie crust into the bottom of a 9-inch pie plate. Pour the prepared apples over the crust and spread evenly. Using your fingers dipped in water, dampen the outer edges of the crust before topping with the remaining crust. Fold and crimp the edges together. Cut four 1-inch slits in the top of the pie. Brush with melted buttter and sprinkle with sugar, if desired.

Place in the oven and bake for 15 minutes. Remove from the oven and cover the entire pie with foil. Cut slits in the center of the foil and peel back so mainly the outer edge is covered (to prevent it from burning). Reduce the heat to 375°F and continue baking for 45 to 55 minutes, until golden.

8 servings

mama's no-fail pecan pie

pecan pie has always been one of our all-time favorites, but it used to be a hit or miss recipe. Sometimes it turned out perfect, but most of the time we had pecan "soup," which we still loved. Mama laughed along with us as we called it that, and she would joke about it as she dished it out into bowls instead of saucers. A friend gave her this recipe when I was a young teen, though, and she announced that Sunday that we were not going to have pecan soup anymore, but pecan pie. Since then, it's been perfect every single time. Although I'd be lying if I said I didn't miss those good old days when Mama would dish soupy pie out into a bowl. . . .

3 eggs

1 cup sugar

½ cup light corn syrup

6 tablespoons (¾ stick) margarine, melted

1 cup pecan halves

One 9-inch unbaked pie shell

In a medium bowl, beat the eggs. Blend in the sugar. Stir in the remaining ingredients and mix well. Pour into the pie shell and place the pie in a cold oven. Turn the oven to 300°F and bake for 1 hour, or until set in the center.

8 servings

candied apples

I still remember when I was a child the magic of coming home from school to see a tray on the counter filled with beautiful shiny candied apples. Mama would smile expectantly as she presented them to us and we'd bite into them with our hearts soaring at such a treat. I can't imagine a more magical confection to a child.

Today most stores sell candied apple kits, but I don't think anything can compare to how good they taste when they are homemade.

3 cups sugar

½ cup light corn syrup

¼ cup cinnamon red hot candies

¼ teaspoon red food coloring

8 wooden ice cream sticks or lollipop sticks

8 small apples

About 2 hours before serving, in a heavy, deep 3-quart saucepan, combine the sugar, corn syrup, candies, red food coloring, and 1 cup water. Place over medium heat and bring to a boil without stirring. Set a candy thermometer in the pan, making sure it does not touch the bottom, and continue cooking, without stirring, until the temperature reaches 290°F, about 20 minutes.

Meanwhile, grease a cookie sheet and insert ice cream sticks or lollipop sticks partway through the stem end of each apple.

When the sugar syrup is ready, remove the pan from the heat. Remove the thermometer. Swirl each apple in the hot cinnamon-candy syrup to coat evenly. Lift out the apples and swirl over the saucepan for a few more seconds to catch the drips.

Place the candy apples on a cookie sheet to cool. If the syrup in the pan begins to stiffen, soften by placing the pan over very low heat. Let the apples cool at least 1 hour before serving. If you just can't wait, the candied apples can be cooled in the refrigerator!

8 servings

slow cooker apple butter

apple butter is surprisingly easy to make, especially with the help of a slow cooker. Still, folks seem to be intimidated by it. Perhaps it's the complex taste of spices combined with how few people actually do make it anymore that causes us to shy away from making it in our own kitchens. There is no need, though, as making apple butter with this recipe is likely one of the easiest things that I've brought to you so far.

I like to put my apple butter on to cook in the slow cooker just before I go to bed and let it cook all night long. When I wake up in the morning, the house is filled with such a delicious and fragrant smell that I often reserve making it for a time when we have company. I wake up first thing, take the lid off, and give it a few fans just to make sure the house is thoroughly saturated with apple butter smell (you might want to save this step until after you've made biscuits, because that breakfast table will fill up pretty quickly!). We eat a breakfast of biscuits and fresh, hot apple butter, while I let the rest continue to cook. This is about as close to heaven as you can possibly get while still drawing breath.

The liquid will evaporate off as you continue to cook it throughout the day, and once it is canned it will thicken even more. This apple butter is going to look like brown applesauce, with a slight grainy texture. I'm always sure to tell this to folks who have never seen apple butter before, lest they think they did something wrong.

Two 3-pound (50-ounce) jars unsweetened applesauce

3 pounds Granny Smith apples

4 cups sugar

1½ cups apple juice

2 teaspoons ground cinnamon

1 teaspoon ground cloves

1 teaspoon ground allspice

Peel and cut the apples into thin slices. Place all the ingredients in a slow cooker and stir. Cover and cook on low overnight (8 to 10 hours). Remove the cover, stir, and taste. Add more spices or sugar if desired. Continue cooking for a few more hours, uncovered, until some of the liquid has gone and the butter has cooked down a bit. Pour into jars and refrigerate (or can it).

Serve over hot biscuits, toast, or scones, or just eat it out of the jar if no one is looking!

about 8 pints

pot o' pintos
(how to cook dried beans)

for most of my life up until now, I have lived within walking distance of a cotton field. I grew up hearing stories of my grandparents working as sharecroppers, growing and picking the cotton in the blazing sun. As a child, I used to have friends who lived just beyond the cotton field in the back of our house, and many a day I'd set out to walk across it, careful to keep to the borders lest I disturb the crop. Have you ever walked through a cotton field after the rain? Thick Alabama clay begins coating your shoes at the first step and continues to pile on until, as you finally reach the other side, you are walking a good three to four inches taller and tennis shoes have turned into red clay–coated space boots that slowly transform back to tennis shoes the farther you get from it, albeit a little worse for wear appearance-wise. On fall days, nothing beats coming back home, knocking off the clay, and walking into the house to be greeted with the smell of pintos simmering on the stove or in the slow cooker. Mama would always make warm cornbread and serve up generous bowls, with extra juice if you asked, to dip your cornbread in—comfort food at its finest.

Dried beans are very inexpensive and make a filling meal when served with bits of ham and a side of Terri's Dixie Cornbread (page 95).

½ **pound dried beans of your choice (my favorites are pinto, navy beans, and black-eyed peas)**

Plenty of water

2 **tablespoons oil or meat grease**

Salt

Pepper

Sugar

Ham bone, ham hock, or bits of leftover ham for seasoning

The night before, sort your beans, place in a pot, and cover with water. Let soak overnight. In the morning, drain the soaking water. Cover with 6 cups fresh water. Add the oil and salt, pepper, and sugar according to taste. A good rule of thumb is to start with a tablespoon of each and then taste it several hours later and add more if you think it needs it. Add one of the following for additional seasoning: a ham hock, ham bone, or slice of country ham. In a pinch, I have actually seasoned my beans with bacon. Bring all of this to a boil, then lower the heat and simmer for several hours. Don't let the water get too low—just add more every few hours as it boils down.

6 to 8 servings

slow cooker cornbread dressing

chicken and dressing is a must-have at holiday and family gatherings in the South. This recipe allows it to be made ahead of time and the mess cleaned up before guests arrive. It also takes the worry of having the dressing come out dry. It always turns out moist and delicious. Serve this with cranberry relish or cranberry sauce from a can.

chicken mixture

1 large chicken, cooked (see Note), deboned, and cut into pieces

One 10.5-ounce can cream of chicken soup, undiluted

Mix the chicken and soup together and set aside.

dressing

1 large skillet cornbread (2 quarts crumbled), see Terri's Dixie Cornbread (page 95)

2 tablespoons dried sage

1 medium onion, chopped

2 hard-boiled eggs, chopped

½ cup (1 stick) margarine, melted

3 to 4 cups chicken broth, from cooking the chicken

One 10-ounce can cream of chicken soup

To make the dressing, mix all the ingredients together, except for the cream of chicken soup. Layer in a slow cooker in the following order: half can cream of chicken soup, half of the dressing mixture, half of the chicken mixture, the remaining dressing, remaining chicken mixture, and remaining cream of chicken soup. Cover and cook on low for 3 hours. Serve hot.

Note: To cook the chicken place in a large saucepan, cover with water, and simmer, covered, until the chicken is tender, approximately 1 hour. Save the broth for the dressing.

8 to 10 servings

streusel-topped pumpkin spice muffins

a neighbor of a friend gave me this recipe when I was telling her about some delicious pumpkin spice muffins I had on a quilting retreat once. Her face immediately lit up with glee as she passed this recipe on to me and informed me that "if you want to make the best pumpkin muffins on earth . . ."

I made them and I agreed—they were sublime—but there is nothing more fun than taking sublime and making it even better. I added my favorite quick and easy streusel topping, and the result was every bit as good (if not better) than something you'd pay an arm and a leg for at your favorite corner coffee shop. Go ahead, impress someone with your culinary skills today. Just make sure you hide the cake mix box in the very bottom of your trash can.

I know, the ingredients just seem too easy for this recipe, but I promise it works. Besides, as busy as you are, easy is never a bad thing.

Any leftover topping can be refrigerated for several weeks or frozen for several months until needed.

muffins

1 box spice cake mix

One 15-ounce can solid-pack pumpkin

½ cup water

Preheat the oven to 350°F. Grease a 12-cup muffin pan.

In a large bowl, combine all the ingredients and mix until well blended. Scoop into the muffin pan.

topping

1 cup all-purpose flour

1 cup brown sugar

½ cup (1 stick) margarine, softened

Make the topping: In a large bowl, stir together the flour and brown sugar, breaking up any lumps. Cut in the margarine. Spoon or sprinkle on top of the muffins, and pat down slightly. Bake for 20 to 24 minutes, or until a toothpick inserted in the center comes out clean.

12 muffins

pumpkin crumb cake

so I heard there was going to be a vast pumpkin shortage. Despite the fact that I only use pumpkin in one recipe, I went right out and bought two cases of canned pumpkin—just in case. We do things like that in my neck of the woods. Now stuck with more pumpkin than I could shake a stick at, I decided I needed to develop another canned pumpkin recipe. This one continues to get great reviews whenever I serve it. I just love crumb cakes!

cake

One 15-ounce can solid-pack pumpkin

2 cups granulated sugar

1 cup milk

2 cups self-rising flour

½ cup (1 stick) margarine

2 eggs

1 teaspoon vanilla extract

1½ teaspoons ground cinnamon

Preheat the oven to 350°F and spray a 9 x 13-inch pan with cooking spray.

Place all the cake batter ingredients in a large bowl and mix until well blended.

crumb topping

½ cup (1 stick) margarine

1 cup brown sugar (dark or light)

1 cup flour (self-rising or all-purpose, whatever you have on hand)

1 cup oats (quick-cooking or old-fashioned)

In a medium bowl, combine all the topping ingredients. Cut together with a long-tined fork until well blended. Pour half of the batter into the pan and top with half of the crumb mixture. Pour the remaining batter over and top with the remaining crumb mixture. Bake for 45 minutes to 1 hour, until a toothpick inserted in the center comes out clean. Serve from the pan.

12 servings

zucchini bread

the first time I ever made zucchini bread was on July 5, 1999. I put it in the oven around 8:05 p.m. Around 8:10, my son decided he was ready to be born. My first thought was "But I just put zucchini bread in the oven!" After a frantic phone call to Mama (who lived just across the street at the time), I left for the hospital, confident that my bread would be taken out of the oven when the timer went off. About seventeen hours later, I was treated to my first taste—and boy, was I hungry by then!

Five and a half years later, when Katy Rose decided to join us, I had just finished making banana bread. I had barely enough time to put a lovely cream cheese glaze on the mini loaves and wrap them to give as gifts to my nurses before heading out.

So I bake quick breads and children appear. Maybe I'm on to something here.

If you have any zucchini left over, measure it out and place it in a freezer bag, making sure to note the amount on the outside of the bag. You don't have to do anything special to it—just peel, shred, and freeze.

3 eggs

¾ cup vegetable oil

2 cups sugar

2 teaspoons vanilla extract

2 cups shredded zucchini

One 8-ounce can crushed pineapple, drained

3 cups all-purpose flour

2 teaspoons baking soda

½ teaspoon baking powder

½ teaspoon salt

1½ teaspoons ground cinnamon

¾ teaspoon ground nutmeg, optional

1 cup chopped nuts

1 cup raisins

Preheat the oven to 350°F and generously grease two 4 x 8-inch loaf pans or four to six mini loaf pans.

In a large bowl, combine the eggs, oil, sugar, vanilla, zucchini, and pineapple. In a separate bowl, sift together the flour, baking soda, baking powder, salt, cinnamon, and nutmeg, if using. Add the nuts and raisins and mix all together.

Pour into the pans and bake for 1 hour for the full-size loaf pans or 30 minutes for the mini loaf pans, or until the centers are no longer soft.

2 loaves

hoe cake

hoe cake seems to be a rather elusive recipe, even among Southerners. Apart from my own family, I have only one friend whose family still makes it.

Even among us, though, the variations are vast. My friend's family makes it using cornmeal, as seems to be the custom among recipes found on the Web. My family's version uses flour and produces a bread much like buttermilk biscuits in flavor, only with a lighter and fluffier texture and crispy outsides.

Either way you look at it, hoe cake is revered by those who are familiar with it. I am sure its origins sprang forth much like the rest of our Southern dishes—too little time and too few ingredients. It is a simple bread to make but will easily take over the starring role at your dinner table.

½ **cup vegetable shortening**

2 **cups self-rising flour (see Note)**

1 **cup milk**

Preheat the oven to 425°F. Pour a thin layer of oil to cover the bottom of an 8-inch round cake pan and place in the oven to heat.

In a large bowl, thoroughly cut the shortening into the flour. Pour the milk in and stir until wet. The batter will be lumpy. Pour into the well-heated pan and bake for 15 to 20 minutes, until browned. Invert onto a plate.

Note: If self-rising flour is not available, simply add 1½ teaspoons baking powder and 1 teaspoon salt to each cup of all-purpose flour to make your own self-rising flour.

8 servings

how to host a gathering
and have a clean kitchen!

I dearly love to have friends and family over to my home, and fall is the prime time of year for hosting gatherings in the South. I'm often asked for ideas when it comes to planning these events, and my goal is for my guests always to enjoy themselves. But, of course, I want to enjoy myself as well. A surefire way to make sure I don't make the most out of my evening is to be stuck in the kitchen or to have a messy kitchen that I'm worried about my guests seeing all night.

What I like to do is plan a menu that has most of the cooking done ahead of time. The following timetable allows you to begin preparations three days before the event, and leaves you relaxed and with a clean kitchen when your guests arrive.

two to three days before the gathering:

shop for all groceries and make dessert. Refrigerator cakes are wonderful for large gatherings because they can be made in advance and rather than getting dry, they actually get better as the days go by. On the day of your event, simply open the fridge and dessert is served.

The following cakes are excellent choices:

Mandarin Orange Cake (page 14)
Daddy's Coconut Cake (page 155)
Butterfinger Cake (page 22)

One cake for every ten people is a good rule of thumb.

one to two days before the gathering:

make your main course. Stews and chilis are great this time of year. More filling than soups, their warmth and meal-in-one convenience can't be beat for serving a crowd. These are all excellent choices for making ahead of time, as they all taste even better once their flavors have had time to blend and develop. A double recipe will easily feed ten people.

Make sure you have hot sauce and crackers. If you are serving chili, make sure you have shredded cheese, sour cream, and any other toppings your family likes.

Aunt Louise's Beef Stew (page 242)
Hamburger Stew (page 111)
Chicken Stew (page 93)
Christy's Chili (page 96)

Allow the stew or chili to cool and store in the refrigerator.

the day of the gathering:

set the buffet or table. Heat up the stew or chili and make bread. Good choices are:

Terri's Dixie Cornbread (page 95)
Hoe Cake (page 132)

Open up your home and enjoy your guests!

christmas

· · · · ·

in the South, Christmas is not just a holiday, it's a season. In fact, it is often said that the South's four seasons are almost summer, summer, still summer, and Christmas! A season filled with parties, celebrations, and food so special that we reserve it only for the holidays.

Even folks who don't enjoy cooking other times of the year are quick to crank out their holiday classics. Fudge, divinity, velvet cakes, peanut brittle, and every cookie imaginable make their way onto party trays and into gift exchanges. Nothing says merry Christmas to a Southerner more than something baked with care and given with love.

This is the season where we take the absolute best of the best, our fanciest food, and deliver it to neighbors on paper plates covered in tinfoil. We're a fun contradiction that way.

christmas recipes

the seven cakes
of christmas

life during the Depression in rural Alabama wasn't too different from any other time for my family. You see, they were sharecroppers—dirt farmers who didn't even own their own dirt. They wouldn't have known if the rest of the world had been prosperous— their lives had always been a struggle of hard work and all too often relying on hope for the next meal.

During the holidays, there wasn't a whole lot to be thankful for, other than the fact that there wasn't any cotton to pick. For them, winter was as bleak as the Alabama landscape. In Alabama, we are not often afforded the sight of glistening snow resting atop hills and trees in a winter wonderland. Here, the sky just gets gray and the landscape browns—bare trees, brown grass, and muddy earth where fields lay in wait for spring . . . as far as the eye can see.

My great-grandmother had four children, and they all lived in a small shack house. Wood was a precious thing, and that meant only heating one room. My grandmama says, "It got so cold at night. Mama would heat rocks and wrap 'em up in old towels to put in bed with us, but we still got so cold. They didn't dare get out of that bed unless they just had to."

Families would work all year for the farm owner in exchange for monthly rations of staples such as dried beans, flour, and the occasional bit of meat. At harvest's end they'd get a percentage of the profits from the cotton, but all of the staples that had been provided for them were then deducted from the final cost, leaving families in a continual state of dependence upon the farm owner for enough food to survive the winter.

But with winter came Christmas, and my great-grandmother always did manage to make it special despite their hardships. Lela's life had always been a hard one. Growing up one of nine children in Jackson County, she spent her childhood traveling from farm to farm with her parents and siblings, picking cotton and tending to whatever crops the farm owner decided to plant. Now she had four kids to provide a Christmas for and keeping them fed and clothed took about all she had and then some.

But she never failed them. She always came through, especially at Christmastime.

Lela squirreled away ingredients all year long. A little sugar here, some dried apples there, maybe some raisins and a bit of cinnamon. After the kids went to bed on Christmas Eve, she'd set to work. Using only what she had on hand and no recipes to speak of, Lela would stay awake all night baking cakes in her little wood stove. She'd make an apple stack cake, a raisin cake, yellow cake with chocolate icing, peanut butter cake, and so on. There was never a plan beyond that of needing to make seven of them—one for each day from Christmas until the New Year.

The next morning, four sets of eyes would open wide and four sets of feet would hurry out of their cold beds into the only heated room in the house where their faces would light up at the sight of seven cakes sitting on the worn kitchen table. I know how their faces looked because my grandmother's still lights up the same way even now, some seventy years later, when she talks about those cakes. The kids took turns being the one to choose the cake they ate that day, and between the six of them and any company who happened by, they made short work of it and were ready to start with a new one the next morning.

Most kids today would consider having cakes baked for you as your only Christmas gift to be a disappointment. But amid all of the wrappings and bows, gift sets and feasts, I hope your Christmas somehow manages to be as magical as it was in that little sharecropper's house in Alabama during the Depression, when four kids woke up with stars in their eyes at finding seven cakes baked just for them.

chocolate velvet cake

this is my little spin on a Southern classic, and the most requested cake by my girl-friends. Deeply chocolate, we add chocolate morsels to dress it up even more and then top it off with a rich cream cheese icing. If I'm taking this to a get-together, I put chocolate sprinkles and little chocolate shavings all over the top. It's just too much to resist!

cake

- 2 heaping tablespoons unsweetened cocoa powder, plus more for dusting the pans
- 1 box any flavor of chocolate cake mix (I use Duncan Hines)
- 1 cup sour cream
- ½ cup milk
- ¼ cup vegetable oil
- 3 eggs
- 1 to 2 teaspoons butter flavoring (you can substitute vanilla extract)
- 1 cup chocolate chips

Preheat the oven to 350°F. Grease two 9-inch cake pans with shortening and dust with cocoa powder.

Combine all the ingredients except the chocolate chips in a large bowl. Mix for about 2 minutes, until well blended. Mix in the chocolate chips. Divide evenly among the prepared pans and bake for about 25 minutes, or until a toothpick inserted in the center comes out clean. Let the cakes cool in the pans for 10 minutes, then turn out onto a wire rack to cool completely before icing the cake.

cream cheese icing

- 8 ounces cream cheese
- ½ cup (1 stick) margarine or butter
- 3½ to 4 cups confectioners' sugar
- 1 to 2 teaspoons butter flavoring (you can substitute vanilla extract)

While the cake is in the oven, make the icing: Soften the cream cheese and margarine by leaving out on a counter until it reaches room temperature. Combine the two in a large bowl and mix until well blended. Add the confectioners' sugar and mix until smooth. Add the butter flavoring and mix some more until well incorporated and the icing is creamy.

12 servings

sugared pecans

these are such a treat to have. I especially love buying them at fairs and festivals in the fall from vendors who are masters at the art of filling the air with the irresistible scent of cinnamon. In the fall, if you can find a good deal on pecans or if you know a generous soul with a pecan tree, these make thoughtful "thinking of you" gifts for friends and neighbors.

They're so incredibly easy to make, I know you'll love them.

1 egg white

1 tablespoon water

1 cup sugar

1 teaspoon salt

1 teaspoon ground cinnamon

2 cups pecan halves

Preheat the oven to 300°F.

In a large bowl, beat the egg white and water until frothy. In a separate bowl, mix the sugar, salt, and cinnamon.

Dip the pecans in the egg mixture, then roll in the sugar mixture (see Note). Put them on a cookie sheet and bake for 30 minutes, stirring halfway through.

Note: Pour just 1 cup of pecans into the egg-water mixture and "dip" out with a slotted spoon. Then put them into the sugar mixture and take out a few at a time with the slotted spoon, shaking the excess sugar back into the remaining sugar mixture. Spread the pecans out on a cookie sheet before baking.

2 cups

candy-coated peanuts

Mama's friend Peggy gave her a bag of these candied peanuts along with the recipe one Christmas, and we instantly took to them. Peggy is from Dothan, Alabama, which is known as the peanut capital of the world. Mama decided that year to make them at the last minute to add to her gift baskets, and everyone she delivered them to asked for the recipe as well.

1 cup sugar
½ cup water
2 cups raw peanuts (skin on)

Preheat the oven to 300°F.

In a medium saucepan, combine the sugar and water. Place over medium heat and stir until the sugar dissolves.

Add the peanuts and continue to cook over medium heat, stirring frequently, until the peanuts are completely sugar-coated and no sugar syrup remains, about 30 minutes.

Pour out onto an ungreased cookie sheet and separate the peanuts with a fork. Bake for 30 minutes, stirring every 10 minutes. Allow to cool on a cookie sheet, then store in a sealed container. Mama stores hers in a mason jar.

2 cups

mexican wedding cookies

when I was a little girl, my favorite cookies were called wedding cookies and were sold in a pink box at the grocery store. We were on a tight budget, though, and store-bought cookies were a rarity in our house. Instead, Mama made me her own version of these, which were better by far. My kids love to help out with this recipe, so I let them dip the warm cookies into the confectioners' sugar.

½ **cup vegetable shortening**

¼ **cup water**

1 **teaspoon vanilla extract**

1 **egg white**

1 **box white cake mix**

½ **cup chopped nuts, optional**

½ **cup mini semisweet chocolate chips**

Confectioners' sugar

Preheat the oven to 375°F. In a large bowl, mix the shortening, water, vanilla, and egg white together thoroughly. Mix in the cake mix, nuts, and chocolate chips until the dough holds together.

Shape into 1-inch balls and place about 2 inches apart on ungreased cookie sheets. Bake until almost set, about 10 minutes. While warm, dip the tops in confectioners' sugar, then cool completely.

5 dozen

lucy's chocolate pie

this has been my brother's favorite pie since he was just a boy. Grandmama makes it every year for Christmas, and we all flock to it. I'm often asked if I have a special chocolate pie recipe, so now you can claim it as your own, a gift from my grandmama. Serve it to those you hold dear.

1 cup sugar or Splenda

⅓ cup unsweetened cocoa powder

¼ cup self-rising flour

2 egg yolks

2 cups milk

2 teaspoons butter or margarine

1 teaspoon vanilla extract

Pinch of salt

1 baked pie shell

Preheat the oven to 325°F.

In a medium saucepan, combine the sugar, cocoa powder, and flour. Mix well. Beat in the egg yolks and add the milk. Place over medium heat and cook until thickened, stirring constantly to prevent scorching. Stir in the butter, vanilla, and salt. Pour into the baked pie shell and top with meringue, if desired, or whipped cream.

meringue

3 egg whites

¼ cup sugar

To make the meringue, whip the egg whites until foamy with an electric mixer on high speed. Add the sugar. Continue beating on high speed until soft peaks form. Pour onto the top of the pie and spread to the edges to seal well. Bake at 325°F for 15 minutes, or until the top is golden. Allow to cool completely and refrigerate before serving if you like.

8 servings

why you're a good mama if your cake is ugly

I try to teach optimism to my kids. I've always felt that teaching children the benefits of a positive attitude is a vital lesson that will benefit them the rest of their lives. I tell them, "Each day when you wake up, you have a choice. You can have a good day or you can have a bad day, so you might as well have a good one." Even at their young ages, they know there is always a brighter side—even if they need help finding it sometimes. They know, above all things, that happiness is a choice. It is not something that comes to you but something you have to reach out and claim each day.

But sometimes it's just not that easy. Sometimes the stresses of the world seem to bear down on us as our minds fill with to-do lists and missed appointments, lost papers, or rapidly growing laundry piles. Sometimes our days feel overwhelming and all we want to do is press the pause button and sit for five minutes with a blank mind. I think mothers are especially prone to this, being the emotional thinkers that we are. We love and therefore we do, but we love so much more than we are capable of doing.

I was having just such a day when I first attempted to write about chocolate velvet cake for Southern Plate. I was excited about sharing a recipe that has always been a hit wherever I take it and decided to do a more involved tutorial, showing my readers exactly how to decorate their cake so that it had a showcase appearance.

My beautiful Katy was so excited about the prospect of cake that she was just about beside herself. My Brady moved his homework operations to the dining room table, where I was decorating, to be closer and to watch me.

As I began taking photos, Katy watched the back of the camera to see them appear on the digital screen. She saw my hands in the photos, and seeing as how she had recently had her fingernails painted, she wanted her hands in the photos, too. Several photos later I finally got through to her that I really needed photos of the cake and not her hands so my readers could see what I was doing. She frowned but complied, and little hands stopped appearing in front of my lens in every shot.

That was when Brady started needing help with his homework . . . and while I was working on that, the smell of cream cheese icing proved too persuasive for my Katy, and little fingers began dipping into the side of the cake. Around about this time, Katy climbed up in a chair to get a better view, and as I stopped her from almost falling out of the chair, I dropped a huge glob of icing right on the carpet. To say I was frazzled would be putting it mildly.

Here I was trying to do a tutorial that I felt was very important, but all my kids wanted was my attention—and my cake. I took the rest of the icing and simply iced the cake, paying no mind to the appearance as I had planned. Then I cut two large slices and placed them in bowls, which I gave to each of my young'uns. The tension in the room dissipated immediately. My kids were absolutely delighted with their bounty, and for the duration of their eating, each one of them kept singing my praises: "Ma, you make the *best* cake!" "This cake is wonderful!" "Mama, I really really like your cake!"

I guess in the end, the kids will not likely remember how the cake looked, but they will remember that you made it for them. And whether it's made from scratch or made from a mix, whether it's chocolate, vanilla, or strawberry, I think when all kids grow up they will agree, their mama made the *best* cake.

old-fashioned sugar plum cake

this is a cherished recipe of my mother's that her mother used to make her as a child, especially at Christmastime. I've always heard her talk about this cake with a longing in her voice, and so I like to surprise her with it from time to time. It's absolutely delicious and so very moist, a true bit of nostalgia from the good old days. This recipe calls for 1 teaspoon nutmeg, but I really don't like nutmeg, so I doubled the cinnamon in its place. If you enjoy nutmeg, substitute 1 teaspoon of it for 1 teaspoon of the cinnamon.

cake

- 2 cups all-purpose flour
- 1½ cups sugar
- 3 eggs
- 1 cup vegetable oil
- 1 teaspoon baking soda
- ½ teaspoon salt
- 1 teaspoon ground allspice
- 2 teaspoons ground cinnamon
- 1 cup buttermilk
- 1 teaspoon vanilla extract
- 1 cup chopped dried plums (see Note)
- 1½ cups chopped nuts (I use walnuts)

sauce

- ½ cup (1 stick) margarine or butter
- 1½ cups sugar
- ½ teaspoon baking soda
- 2 teaspoons vanilla extract
- ½ cup buttermilk

Preheat the oven to 350°F and grease and flour a Bundt or 9 x 13-inch cake pan.

Combine all the cake ingredients in a large bowl and beat with an electric mixer until well combined. Pour into the cake pan and bake for 1 hour, or until the center springs back when lightly pressed.

Note: Dried plums are more commonly known as prunes, but folks don't take to prunes nowadays like they used to, so we're going to call them dried plums. Hey, whatever it takes to get you through the day!

Just before the cake is done, place all the sauce ingredients into a saucepan. Bring to a boil over medium heat, stirring constantly, and continue boiling gently until the sauce is thickened, about 2 minutes. Remove the fully baked cake from the oven and poke holes all over the top with a fork. Pour the hot sauce over the hot cake. Allow to sit in the pan until the sauce is absorbed. Serve from the pan.

12 servings

pumpkin pie dip

this is a delicious way to use pumpkin pie filling. Mama likes to serve this in the center of a tray at holiday get-togethers with gingersnaps spread out around it.

8 ounces cream cheese

2 cups confectioners' sugar

One 15-ounce can pumpkin pie filling

1½ teaspoons ground cinnamon

½ teaspoon ground ginger

In a large bowl, beat the cream cheese and confectioners' sugar at medium speed with a hand mixer. Add the pie filling, cinnamon, and ginger and beat well. Cover and chill. Serve with gingersnaps and apple slices.

3 cups

holly jollies

this is just about the handiest little Christmas candy you could ever hope to make and really saves the day when holiday schedules get as hectic as they do! Simply start with almond bark (sometimes called candy coating) and choose your favorite add-in. I like to make five or six varieties and use different mini muffin papers to differentiate. I make little gift bags for everyone with an assortment, and it's always been a huge hit. When I put this up on Southern Plate, it became the most blogged-about post in the history of the site. Package and give with a smile on your face and a grateful heart.

1 **package almond bark (white or chocolate) (see Note)**

36 **mini muffin papers**

2 **cups of one or more of the following (get creative!):**

Salted peanuts

Salted cashews

Rice Krispies cereal

Dried cranberries

Raisins

Chocolate-coated candies

Other salted nuts

Your favorite dried fruit, chopped to the size of raisins

Line mini muffin tins with mini muffin papers (you'll need 36 holes).

Place the almond bark in a large microwave-safe bowl. Microwave for 1½ minutes and stir. Return to the microwave and microwave for about 30 seconds at a time, stirring each time, until the bark is smooth and creamy.

Remove from the microwave and stir in 2 cups of your choice of add-in. Spoon into the mini muffin papers and allow to sit until cool and hardened. You can put them in the refrigerator to speed up the process if you like.

Note: Almond bark is just imitation chocolate candy coating. It can be found in the baking aisle and is sometimes sold under the name "candy coating." Despite the name, there are no nuts in almond bark.

36 pieces

daddy's coconut cake

this is my dad's favorite cake at Christmastime and Easter, and it's divine beyond compare. Another great refrigerator cake, it can be made three days ahead of time and then left to sit in the fridge as it grows moister with every passing minute.

1 box yellow cake mix

2 cups sugar

16 ounces sour cream

1½ cups whipped topping

12 ounces shredded sweetened coconut (you can use frozen, bagged, or canned)

Prepare the cake mix according to the package directions in a 9 x 13-inch pan.

While the cake is in the oven, make the icing: Combine the sugar, sour cream, whipped topping, and coconut. Blend well and chill until the cake is ready.

Cool the cake for about 10 minutes, then poke holes all over the top of the still-warm cake. Pour the icing over the cake.

Cover well and refrigerate for 1 to 3 days before serving. Store in the refrigerator.

12 servings

cookie jar christmas cookies

throughout my childhood, these were our must-have cookies for Christmas. Mama would make a huge batch so we all had plenty to decorate. She cut them in the shapes of trees, stars, and reindeer, and each of us got our own platter. She mixed up red, green, and yellow icing and always had plenty of sprinkles to go on top. They will be "wet" right after icing and decorating; wait an hour or so and they will be dry enough to be stacked in a cookie jar.

This cookie isn't very sweet on its own, which makes it altogether perfect once you add the icing.

Mama always made three batches of icing for these cookies so she could have three different colors. She prefers to use squirt margarine in place of butter for easier blending.

cookies

- ⅔ **cup shortening**
- ¾ **cup granulated sugar**
- ½ **teaspoon vanilla extract**
- 1 **egg**
- 4 **teaspoons milk**
- 2 **cups all-purpose flour**
- 1½ **teaspoons baking powder**
- ¼ **teaspoon salt**

Preheat the oven to 375°F and grease 2 cookie sheets.

In a large bowl, thoroughly cream the shortening, sugar, and vanilla. Add the egg and beat until fluffy. Stir in the milk. Sift the dry ingredients into a separate bowl. Stir the dry ingredients into the wet and blend. Divide the dough in half, wrap in plastic, and chill for 1 hour.

On a floured surface, roll half of the dough to ⅛ inch thick. Keep the remaining dough chilled until ready to roll. Cut into shapes of your choosing and place on the cookie sheets. Bake for 6 to 8 minutes. Cool slightly, then remove the cookies from the pan. Cool completely.

icing

- 1 **cup confectioners' sugar**
- 1 **tablespoon softened butter or margarine**
- 2 **tablespoons milk**
- 1 **teaspoon vanilla extract or butter flavoring**
- **A few drops of food coloring**

While the cookies are cooling, make the icing: In a medium bowl, mix all the ingredients together with a fork. If it's too dry, add a little more milk. Add the food coloring.

2 dozen

cranberry banana bread

I love making quick breads to give away. They make the perfect little gift and are always appreciated, especially at Christmastime. A few years back, I decided to try tossing some dried cranberries into our super-moist banana bread recipe, and this recipe was born. My mother instantly fell in love with it, and it has been a regular holiday recipe ever since.

I really like mini loaves of bread and seldom make full-size ones. In this recipe, you can make two full-size loaves or eight minis. That means eight lucky folks can get this delicious bread from you as a special holiday treat!

3 bananas, peeled

2 cups sugar

½ cup (1 stick) margarine

2 eggs

1 cup milk

3 cups self-rising flour

1 teaspoon vanilla extract

One 6-ounce package dried cranberries

1 cup chopped nuts, optional

Preheat the oven to 350°F and grease and flour 2 loaf pans or 8 mini loaf pans.

Place the bananas in a large bowl and add the sugar. Mix until the bananas are liquefied. Add the margarine and mix until creamed together with the banana mixture. Add all the other ingredients and blend well. Pour into the loaf pans and bake for 1 hour for regular loaf pans or 30 minutes for mini loaf pans. The bread is done when a toothpick inserted in the center comes out clean.

2 loaves

creole candy

this recipe was given to us by a friend from New Orleans and is very similar to a praline. We like to make them in little mini muffin papers, but you can simply drop spoonfuls onto wax paper if you prefer. They are a beautiful addition to any gift basket, but I also like to put some in a clear cellophane bag and tie it up with ribbons to send to teachers as a little "thinking of you" gift. I don't think we can ever thank our teachers enough.

One 1-pound box confectioners'
   sugar

½ cup (1 stick) butter (do not
   substitute margarine)

⅛ teaspoon salt

2 cups pecan halves

½ cup boiling water

1 teaspoon vanilla extract

In a large saucepan, combine all the ingredients except the vanilla. Place over medium heat, bring to a boil, then reduce the heat slightly and continue cooking, stirring only enough to prevent scorching, to the soft-ball stage, 238°F on a candy thermometer. Remove from the heat, add the vanilla, and stir until the mixture begins to thicken.

Pour 1 teaspoon of the mixture into each of 36 tiny muffin papers. Allow to cool completely.

36 pieces

lucy's coffee can bonbons

when I was a little girl, Grandmama always made these at Christmastime but at no other time of the year. She would save large coffee tins throughout the year and then at Christmas fill them up with these amazing bonbons to deliver to her friends and family. We always kept our coffee tin in the refrigerator, and I can remember as a girl opening it up and seeing that tin there, slipping off the lid and sneaking my hand inside to pull back a handful of bonbons. What a treat!

I hardly ever make these because I still just can't seem to help myself around them. So if you make some and plan on seeing me anytime soon, please bring me one . . . or two.

2 **pounds confectioners' sugar**

One 14-ounce can (1⅔ cups) **sweetened flaked coconut**

2 **cups chopped pecans**

One 14-ounce can **sweetened condensed milk**

½ **cup (1 stick) margarine, melted**

1 **package chocolate almond bark, for coating**

In a large bowl, mix all the ingredients except the almond bark well with your hands and form into balls with damp hands. Place on cookie sheets and refrigerate. Melt the chocolate bark by heating in the microwave at 30-second intervals, stirring after each, until completely melted. Dip the bonbons into the topping with a toothpick. Refrigerate before serving.

Note: Be careful to use very dry utensils when working with almond bark or any candy coating. The smallest drop of water will cause it to clot. See page 153 for an explanation of what almond bark is.

forty-eight 1-inch balls

microwave peanut brittle

a modern spin on an old-fashioned treat, this is another one of my daddy's favorites (it's our family's favorite peanut brittle) and is really quick and easy to make. Make sure you don't use a plastic bowl, as this mixture gets too hot for them. This is one of the few recipes you shouldn't make with children, as it gets far too hot for them to safely help with.

1 cup sugar

1 cup raw peanuts, with or without skins

½ cup light corn syrup

⅛ teaspoon salt

1 teaspoon margarine

1 teaspoon vanilla extract

1 teaspoon baking soda

Butter a cookie sheet and set aside.

Mix the sugar, peanuts, corn syrup, and salt together in a large microwave-safe bowl. Microwave on high for 5 minutes. Stir, then microwave on high for 2 more minutes. Stir, then microwave on high for another 2 minutes.

Stir in the margarine and vanilla until well blended. Add the baking soda and stir until light and foamy. Pour onto the buttered cookie sheet and let cool for about 1 hour. Break into pieces.

approximately 1-pound candy

decadent fudge

my husband gets to be the top dog whenever he goes to a conference because I always make several batches of fudge to send with him. Not only does this make him look good but it ensures his popularity, too! Most folks only make fudge at Christmastime, but I tend to make it year-round as special gifts that delight even more out of season. This recipe is quick, easy, and foolproof—provided you can read your candy thermometer. Half the time I can't make out those little numbers but have always gotten compliments on my fudge regardless.

3 cups sugar

⅔ cup evaporated milk

1½ sticks (¾ cup) margarine

One 12-ounce package flavored chips (see Notes)

1½ cups marshmallow cream (see Notes)

½ teaspoon vanilla extract

½ cup pecans or other nuts, chopped, optional (I leave them out)

Grease a 9 x 13-inch baking pan.

Combine the sugar, milk, and margarine in a heavy saucepan over medium heat. Heat to boiling, then stir constantly for about 5 minutes, until the mixture reaches the soft-ball stage—238°F—this is really important.

Remove the pan from the heat. Add the remaining ingredients and stir vigorously until well blended. Pour into the baking pan. Cool (refrigerating is even better), then cut into squares.

Each batch makes 3 pounds.

Notes: For peanut butter fudge, use peanut butter chips. For chocolate fudge, use Nestle Toll House Semi-Sweet Chocolate Morsels. For cinnamon fudge, use cinnamon chips.

You can use marshmallows in place of marshmallow cream, so if you can't find the cream just get a bag of little marshmallows. We are using 7 ounces of marshmallow cream, so I just eyeball and use a little over half of a 12-ounce package of mini marshmallows in its place.

3 pounds candy

lucy's fruit salad

my grandmother has been making this fruit salad for more than fifty years, ever since Miss Cherry gave her the recipe back in 1956. No other desserts exist for me when this one is present. You can tempt me with velvet cake, tiramisù, carrot cake, even Grandmama's chocolate pie, but this fruit salad is the beginning and end as far as I am concerned. For those watching their sugar, Splenda may be substituted, as can sugar-free fruit cocktail.

6 oranges

6 apples

1½ cups red seedless grapes

One 15-ounce can fruit cocktail

6 egg yolks

1½ cups sugar

Peel the oranges and apples. Cut up in small pieces over a bowl so the juice will be saved. Slice the grapes in half and place in the bowl. Add the fruit cocktail.

Drain off the juice from the fruit into a medium saucepan. Add the egg yolks and sugar. Place over medium heat and cook, stirring constantly, until slightly thickened. Remove from the heat and cool completely. Pour over the fruit and chill before serving. Top with whipped cream, if desired. The fruit salad will keep in the refrigerator for several days.

12 to 14 servings

why i don't need
diamonds

there is something about Christmas that makes us pull all we hold dear close to our hearts. Though the holiday may seem to focus on material things at the onset, most of us quickly see right through the commercial aspects of Christmas to the underlying purpose of simply showing those we love how much they mean to us. Christmas Day serves as a reminder of all of the gifts we enjoy each day in our lives, things that are far too grand ever to fit inside a box or stocking.

It's this affirmation of values and sentiment, of the true meaning and wealth of our lives, that helps to get us centered the rest of the year. So today, in light of all of this, I'm thinking about diamonds. Stay with me now—it'll all make sense in the end.

About twelve years ago, I met the man I wanted to marry. Fortunately for him, he had the good sense to want to marry me, too. He was in his last semester of college, I was right smack dab in the middle of getting my degree, and we lived in two different states. Now when you meet the person you want to marry, living in two different states simply won't do. So as soon as he got closer to graduation, we made plans to get married so that we could remedy the problem.

The day we went ring shopping, neither one of us was focused on "the ring," but instead on what it symbolized for us. I knew roughly what shape I wanted, but that was about it. We walked into the store and glanced around, looking over all of the cases with our stomachs in knots. Some folks thought we were marrying too soon, but we were confident that this was what we wanted to do. I was concerned about finances, having no desire to go into debt immediately and also wanting to make sure folks didn't think I had looked around merely to pluck up the first promising graduate I could find (it is humorous now, me worrying over people thinking I was a gold digger, I know). After a few minutes, I led Ricky over to the case of cubic zirconium and there I saw the most beautiful set of rings I'd ever laid eyes upon.

The entire set cost around $200, which is a drop in the bucket compared to what most sets cost nowadays, but even now, I consider that expensive. They were both placed on my finger August 8, 1998, and I have never been so proud to wear a piece of jewelry. The original plan was to replace the them with diamonds later on, but over the years, that ring began to mean even more to me. It became a symbol of my own value system. Sentiment and meaning—where the heart was in the giving of the ring itself—far outweighed what a jeweler would call the stones.

When Brady was a baby, he used to toy around with the rings, sliding them around on my fingers and oohing and ahhing at how they sparkled. One day as he got older he asked me what I was going to do with them "when I grew up," and I told him that if he wanted, he could have them one day. His face beamed and sparkled every bit as much as my rings did at hearing that.

When Katy was born, I had a bad habit of accidentally scratching her with the rings and so I took them off for a bit, only to dazzle her when she was out of diapers by beginning to wear them again. To her they were magical jewels that just appeared on her mother's hand one day and she, too, took to turning them around, watching them sparkle with delight just as her brother had done at the same age.

I've worn them for years, sometimes taking them off and placing them in my jewelry box for days or even weeks at a time as life calls me away to extensive cooking or housework, but I always come back to them and pull them out, thinking of how beautiful my rings are and how lucky I am to have just this one particular set—the prettiest I've ever seen.

One day my kids will have these rings, the ones they've spent their childhood seeing on my left hand. They'll have grown up knowing what a treasure they are and the meaning behind them, and I can't imagine them wishing "real" diamonds into the settings any more than I would.

mini cheesecakes

these are so pretty at Christmas parties and the perfect little size for finger foods. We make ours with cherry pie filling and put a little cherry on top of each one, but you can get creative and use blueberry pie filling or another of your choice.

¾ **cup graham cracker crumbs**

2 **tablespoons butter or margarine, softened**

¼ **cup plus 1 tablespoon sugar**

One 8-ounce package **cream cheese, at room temperature**

1 **egg**

½ **teaspoon vanilla extract**

Pie filling (cherry or blueberry), for serving

Preheat the oven to 350°F and line mini muffin pans with 36 mini muffin papers.

In a medium bowl, mix the graham cracker crumbs with the butter and 1 tablespoon of sugar. Put 1 teaspoon of the mixture in each mini muffin paper and press down with your finger.

In a separate bowl, cream the cream cheese and remaining ¼ cup sugar together. Mix in the egg and vanilla.

Spoon the mixture into the muffin papers until the muffin papers are half full. Bake for 10 to 12 minutes, or until set. Let cool completely, then refrigerate. Before serving, top each with a small amount of pie filling.

36 mini cheesecakes

pecan pie muffins

this is a gem of a recipe that was passed around our sewing group. Dense little muffins with the taste of pecan pie, they have very few ingredients and are a breeze to turn out. Readers always remark on the rave reviews they get, and they've become a standard for everyone who has ever tried them.

1 cup chopped pecans

1 cup brown sugar (dark or light)

½ cup all-purpose flour

2 eggs

½ cup (1 stick) butter or margarine, melted

Preheat the oven to 350°F and line muffins pans with baking cups to fill 9 holes. Coat with cooking spray.

Combine the pecans, sugar, and flour in a large bowl and make a well in the center of the mixture. In a separate bowl, beat the eggs until foamy. Add the butter, then add to the dry ingredients, stirring until just moistened.

Spoon the batter into the baking cups, filling two-thirds full. Bake for 20 to 25 minutes, until a toothpick inserted in the center comes out clean. Remove from the pans immediately.

9 muffins

tookie's green velvet cake

according to our dear family friend (whose nickname is Tookie), the secret to her red velvet cake is that you make the layers ahead of time and freeze them. You can start making and freezing the layers as early as October and then pull them out and ice them all when the holiday season arrives. Out of all the red velvet cakes we've tried, Tookie's recipe is by far the best. In our family, the tradition changes a bit. You see, my Grandmother Lucille is allergic to red food dye, so our velvet cakes are always green.

cake

2½ cups all-purpose flour

1 teaspoon unsweetened cocoa powder

1 teaspoon baking soda

1 teaspoon salt

1½ cups granulated sugar

1 cup buttermilk

1½ cups vegetable oil

2 eggs

1 teaspoon vinegar

1 teaspoon vanilla extract

One 1-ounce bottle green food coloring

Preheat the oven to 350°F and grease and flour two 9-inch round cake pans.

In a medium bowl, stir together the flour, cocoa powder, baking soda, and salt.

In a large bowl, mix together the sugar, buttermilk, oil, eggs, and vinegar. Add the dry mixture to the wet mixture. Beat on medium speed until well blended. Add the vanilla and green food coloring and beat on low speed until blended. Pour into the cake pans and bake until a toothpick inserted in the center comes out clean, 25 to 30 minutes. Allow to cool 10 minutes in the pan before turning out to cool completely.

icing

One 8-ounce package cream cheese, at room temperature

½ cup (1 stick) margarine, at room temperature

1 pound confectioners' sugar

1 teaspoon vanilla extract

1 cup chopped pecans, optional

While the cake is in the oven, make the icing: Cream together the cream cheese and margarine. Add the confectioners' sugar, vanilla, and nuts, if using. Mix until spreading consistency. A few drops of milk can be added if needed. Frost the cake.

12 servings

Southerners and Nicknames

If you're a Southerner and anyone has ever loved you at all, chances are you've got a nickname. My brother still answers to Sugar Booger, while my sister is Patti Rat. Me, I'm Poochie, a nickname given to me on the day I was born by my brother (Sugar Booger), who took one look at me, spit on me, and declared that I was ugly, "just like a poochie dog."

Only in the South can a name with such origins turn into a beloved term of endearment. I hardly recall my daddy saying "Christy"; it's always "Pooch" or "Poochie." Friends who have known me the longest call me that more than my given name. Do I mind? Goodness, no! I can't think of a better sign that I'm loved.

microwave chex mix

everyone has their own take on this favorite munching treat, and this is mine. I tweaked Grandmama's recipe just a bit but kept her easy preparation method. And it's best if made a day in advance. After all, who has time to fuss over things right before a party?

½ cup (1 stick) margarine

2 teaspoons seasoned salt

3 tablespoons Worcestershire sauce

1 cup mixed nuts

8 cups assorted Chex cereal (you can use one kind or combine two of your favorites)

Place the margarine, seasoned salt, and Worcestershire sauce in a large microwave-safe bowl. Heat in the microwave just until melted. Stir in the nuts, then the cereal. Microwave for 2 minutes, stir, then microwave for 2 minutes more. Stir, then microwave a final 2 minutes, stir, and eat! The mix will be soft until it cools and then it will be nice and crunchy.

eight 1-cup servings

grandmama's tex-mex dip

this is Grandmama's special layered dip that she makes every year at Christmastime on the day we have our big family get-together. As soon as you walk in the door, the dip is sitting on the table ready to be eaten.

2 medium ripe avocados

1 tablespoon lemon juice

½ teaspoon salt

½ teaspoon black pepper

½ cup sour cream

¼ cup mayonnaise

½ package taco seasoning

One 16-ounce can bean dip

½ bunch green onions, chopped

2 medium tomatoes

3 ounces chopped ripe olives

½ cup shredded sharp cheddar cheese

Tortilla chips

Peel, pit, and mash the avocados in a medium bowl. Add the lemon juice, salt, and pepper.

In a small bowl, combine the sour cream, mayonnaise, and taco seasoning. Mix well.

Spread the bean dip on a large, shallow platter. Top with the avocado mixture, then the sour cream mixture. Sprinkle with the chopped green onions, then the tomatoes and olives. Cover with the shredded cheese. Refrigerate until ready to serve. Serve with tortilla chips.

8 to 10 servings

aunt sue's microwave divinity

no Southern Christmas would be complete without divinity, a traditional candy closely resembling a white fudge. Aunt Sue's recipe is a lot easier than traditional ones. Make sure you don't try to make it on a rainy day, though, as it will not set correctly. Mama says, "You just need a clear and pretty day to have pretty divinity!" It's best to use a stand mixer to make this, as it frees up your hands and saves your arms as well. I've lost count of how many hand mixers I've burned up making divinity because it gets stiff and very hard to beat toward the end.

Some folks like to leave the nuts out and simply place a pecan half on top of each piece before it cools. This makes for a pretty presentation.

2¼ cups sugar

½ cup water

½ cup light corn syrup

¼ teaspoon salt

2 egg whites

1½ teaspoons vanilla extract

½ cup chopped pecans

Mix together the sugar, water, corn syrup, and salt in a 2-quart heatproof casserole dish. Loosely cover with a piece of microwave-safe plastic wrap. Microwave for 6 minutes, then uncover and microwave for 9 more minutes.

While the syrup is cooking for the last 9 minutes, beat the egg whites on high speed until stiff. Slowly pour the hot syrup in a small stream over the egg whites while continuing to beat at high speed. Add the vanilla (use clear vanilla so the divinity will be nice and white) and continue beating on high speed for another 4 to 5 minutes, until the mixture holds its shape. Fold in the nuts quickly.

Quickly drop teaspoonfuls of the mixture onto wax paper and let cool.

36 pieces

chocolate cobbler mix

this is a wonderful and intriguing mix to give at Christmastime to anyone who has never heard of chocolate cobbler. The full recipe and story behind it can be found on page 94.

1 cup self-rising flour

¾ cup granulated sugar

2 tablespoons unsweetened cocoa powder

½ cup chopped nuts

¾ cup brown sugar

¼ cup unsweetened cocoa powder

Combine the flour, sugar, cocoa powder, and nuts in an airtight plastic bag and seal. Label it #1. Combine the brown sugar and cocoa powder in a second airtight plastic bag. Label it #2. Place both bags in a gift container or box and attach the following instructions for baking: Combine package #1 with ½ cup milk, 1 teaspoon vanilla extract, and 2 tablespoons vegetable oil. Pour into a greased 8 x 8-inch pan.

Sprinkle package #2 over the batter. Pour (very slowly) 1¾ cups hot tap water over the dry mixture and batter. Bake at 350°F for 40 to 45 minutes.

makes 1 mix

Gift-Giving Mixes

In the age of outlandish holidays with ever-growing price tags, just about everyone appreciates a heartfelt gift personally made for them. Gift mixes are an excellent way of doing this.

Baked goods are always well liked, but mixes offer even more time-saving convenience on the part of the giver and give the receiver an opportunity to have some special time in their kitchen. Even people who work full-time outside the home can squeeze in time to prepare a special treat if they have a mix.

chocolate chip pie mix

Mama received this mix for Christmas one year, and we all fell in love with this pie. It is very similar to the pie made famous in Louisville, Kentucky. If you haven't ever tried a piece, you are in for a wonderful treat.

1 cup sugar

½ cup all-purpose flour

1 cup (6 ounces) Nestle Toll House Semi-Sweet Chocolate Morsels

½ cup sweetened flaked coconut

½ cup chopped pecans

Combine the sugar and flour in an airtight plastic bag and seal. Put the chocolate chips, coconut, and pecans in a second airtight plastic bag. Place both bags in a gift container or box and attach the following directions for baking:

Combine ¼ cup melted butter, the dry ingredient package, and 2 large eggs. Stir until the dry ingredients are moistened. Stir in the chocolate chip package. Spoon into an unbaked 9-inch pie crust. Bake at 350°F for 35 to 40 minutes.

makes 1 mix

hot chocolate mix

when I was a child, we used to mix up a batch of this at the start of each winter and it would last the entire season. I enjoy letting my kids mix it up and then packaging it into little kits to give as "snowman soup," another great gift idea for classmates, friends, family, or anyone else your children would like to offer a special thank you to.

This hot chocolate mix was originally made in my first-grade class. With my teacher Mrs. Menotti, we mixed it all together and each had a cup of hot chocolate. I came home with the instructions and proudly announced to my mother that I had learned to cook! We immediately had to go out for the ingredients and make more to give to family. I stood back to watch their reactions as each tried my recipe.

Present this nicely by packaging the mix in a plastic bag, putting it into a pretty mug, and trying it up with a decorative ribbon to match the mug. Attach the instructions by punching a hole and running a ribbon through it.

1 pound confectioners' sugar

One 8-quart box instant powdered milk

One 6-ounce package powdered coffee creamer

One 2-pound box powdered chocolate milk mix

Sift the confectioners' sugar into a large bowl. Mix in the remaining ingredients. Divide into 1-cup servings and place in airtight plastic bags. Seal. Attach the following instructions:

Fill a mug one-third full with hot chocolate mix. Fill with hot water. Stir and enjoy!

64 servings

chocolate gravy mix

this mix always gets oohs and aahs when given to family and friends and makes a special treat on Christmas morning. The story behind Chocolate Gravy and the original recipe may be found on page 213.

1 cup sugar

2 teaspoons all-purpose flour

1 tablespoon unsweetened cocoa powder

Mix all the ingredients together, place in an airtight plastic bag, and seal. Attach the following instructions:

In a medium saucepan, combine this package with 1¼ cups milk. Bring to a boil over medium heat, stirring constantly to prevent scorching. Turn down the heat and stir for a minute more (it will get pretty thick rather suddenly). Take off the heat and stir in 1 teaspoon butter or margarine.

Serve over hot biscuits for an old-fashioned treat, just like your grandmother made.

Note: This also fits perfectly in an 8-ounce jar.

makes 1 mix

fruit crisp mix

I like to package this mix along with a 29-ounce can of peaches so all the receiver has to add is a stick of margarine or butter. You can also make it with fresh fruit. Often I let my kids color their own labels for the peach can and we tape them on for a more personalized and fun gift.

½ **cup flour (all-purpose or self-rising)**

¾ **cup brown sugar**

½ **cup oats (quick-cooking or old-fashioned)**

1 **teaspoon ground cinnamon**

One **29-ounce can sliced peaches**

Mix all the dry ingredients together in a large bowl until well blended. Place in an airtight plastic bag and seal. Package with the can of peaches and the following instructions:

Pour the mix into a bowl and cut in ⅓ cup softened butter or margarine. Place 2 cups of drained fruit in an 8 x 8-inch baking dish and sprinkle the dry mixture over the top. Bake at 350°F for 30 minutes, or until lightly browned. Serve warm, with ice cream.

makes 1 mix

spring

. . . . .

come springtime, gardens are being planted and we're all itching for that first green tomato to bring in and fry up for supper. As much as we complain about the heat of summer, we sure are ready for it after just a few months of overcast skies and sweaters!

Spring hosts a slew of bridal and baby showers, along with our special Easter dinners. Everyone comes out in their Sunday best to gather together amid picnic tables and daffodils, all hankering for a bite of something fresh and light to go along with a serving of sunshine!

Fruits, vegetables, and all manner of congealed salads are rolled out beneath the spring sunshine as we draw together once more to celebrate family and heritage with our favorite dishes of the season.

spring recipes

homemade ice cream

Grandmama and Granddaddy made homemade ice cream when their strawberries started coming in, and there was nothing like it. This recipe is delicious on its own, but you can easily add your favorite chopped fresh fruit for an even more delicious treat.

6 **pasteurized eggs**

1½ **cups sugar**

1 **pint whipping cream**

One 14-ounce can condensed milk

1 **teaspoon vanilla extract**

Whole milk

In a large bowl, beat the eggs and sugar well with a wire whisk. Add the whipping cream, condensed milk, and vanilla. Stir well to blend. Pour into a 2-quart ice cream freezer and add milk to the fill line.

Freeze according to directions on your ice cream freezer and enjoy! Two cups fresh sweetened fruit may be added before freezing.

½ gallon

frozen cranberry banana salad

creamy, fruity, light-tasting, and just the right size when prepared in a little muffin paper, this is the quintessential tearoom must-have and a very special treat to enjoy at home.

This recipe came from my husband's grandmother, Granny Jordan. She was the embodiment of everything a Southern lady should be. Practically any time guests happened by, she would be prepared with a warm welcome and plenty of Southern hospitality, thanks to these little delights.

Once you make them, simply remove the muffin papers from your pans, pop them into zipper-seal freezer bags, and have an instant company-worthy dessert or special treat for yourself anytime.

One 20-ounce can crushed pineapple, well drained

1 pint sour cream

9 ounces whipped topping

4 bananas, mashed

½ cup sugar

1 cup nuts, optional

Two 16-ounce cans whole cranberry sauce (make sure they are whole)

In a large bowl, mix all the ingredients well and spoon into cupcake papers placed in a muffin pan. Freeze. When frozen, remove the papers from the muffin pan, place in a freezer bag, and seal. Store in the freezer until ready to serve.

24 servings

french breakfast puffs

just about everyone I know has a version of this recipe, and we all call them something different. In case you don't have one yet, this is my recipe. You're going to love the soft doughnut-like texture and buttery topping. These are even better later on in the day, so I like to make a double batch and take them to friends (saving a few for myself!).

½ cup shortening

1 cup sugar

1 egg

1½ cups self-rising flour

¼ teaspoon ground nutmeg (see Note)

½ cup milk

1 teaspoon ground cinnamon

½ cup (1 stick) margarine, melted

Preheat the oven to 350°F and grease 15 medium muffin cups.

In the bowl of an electric mixer, beat the shortening, ½ cup of the sugar, and the egg thoroughly. Mix in the flour and nutmeg alternately with the milk.

Fill the muffin cups two-thirds full and bake for 20 to 25 minutes, until golden brown.

In a small bowl, mix the remaining ½ cup sugar and the cinnamon together. Immediately after baking, dip the puff tops in the melted margarine and then in the sugar mixture. Serve hot.

Note: I love these muffins but truly dislike nutmeg. I leave it out in this recipe.

15 puffs

listenin'
to the old folks

I was raised to listen to the old folks. Mama and Daddy taught me that if someone older than you wants to share a bit of wisdom or tell you a story about the old days, you sit down and accept the gift. And so I have, all of my life. I was blessed to have a wealth of "old folks" around me as a child and even now, to share stories, lessons they've learned, and little nuggets that I will always carry with me.

Their generosity has forever altered the course of my life.

Its easy to see, then, why I can't understand how others do not see the wealth among them. Most folks will tell you that our greatest natural resource is our children, and while I'm a parent who loves her children dearly, I could not disagree more with that statement. Children may be our future, but the real resource is not so much those who are heading forward but those who are returning from the journey—the folks who are able to draw the maps.

What greater treasure can you hope for but the wisdom of someone who walked the same path before you. Oh, sure, you may think that life is drastically different today than it used to be, but really, the essence is the same. The meaning is the same, we just have fancier accessories. We're kidding ourselves if we think we're so special that the basic lessons and wisdom of life are rendered obsolete.

The most essential wisdom of life can only be gained from those older than us, our senior citizens. The folks whose faces we sometimes overlook amid the shiny, pulsing sparkle of youth. They walk at a slower pace, their eyes busy noticing details that escape our hurried glances, and their gait one of quiet wisdom, knowing that life does not move with the ebb and flow of our schedules but with the giving and taking of breaths.

Each day, we're surrounded by these amazing people. Show them the respect they deserve. Look upon their kind eyes and wrinkled skin with awe. Take a moment to get to know them, to return their smile and slow down enough to allow them to speak.

Whether you are raising kids, choosing a career, or just struggling through the daily business of life, if you're moving into the place they once occupied in this world, it only makes sense to ask them for the key.

lemon meringue pie

lemon pie is a staple in the South, especially in the hotter months. Often referred to as "lemon icebox pie," it is commonly kept in the fridge and served cold as a refreshing ending to any meal. Of course, you can purchase a lemon meringue pie at any grocery store and most fast-food chains, but once you've had it made from scratch, all store-bought versions will pale in comparison.

This is a surprisingly simple pie to make, even with the homemade cookie crumb crust. Feel free, though, to use a store-bought crust. Those who don't care for meringue can leave the pie "topless" or add whipped topping in its place once the pie has baked and cooled.

crust

1 box vanilla wafers

3 tablespoons sugar

6 tablespoons margarine

Preheat the oven to 325°F. Crush half of the wafers (about 40). Stir in the sugar. Add the melted margarine and stir until well blended. Pat out into a pie plate.

filling

One 14- or 15-ounce can sweetened condensed milk

½ cup lemon juice (fresh or bottled)

2 egg yolks

To make the filling, mix all the ingredients with an electric mixer until well blended. Pour into the crust.

meringue

3 egg whites

¼ cup sugar

To make the meringue, whip the egg whites until foamy with an electric mixer on high speed. Add the sugar. Continue beating on high speed until soft peaks form. Pour onto the top of the pie and spread to the edges to seal well. Bake at 325°F for 15 minutes, or until the top is golden. Allow to cool completely and refrigerate before serving if you like.

8 servings

homemade cinnamon buns

these cinnamon rolls have power behind them—real power. You could pretty much get anything you wanted if you showed up toting a plate of these babies, warm with icing oozing down the side. Regardless of their power, though, I want you to try to use them only for good. Rather than taking over the world (which I am waiting to do once I get both kids in school), these cinnamon rolls make wonderful gifts of gratitude and tokens of caring. I especially love that I can make them ahead of time and put them in the fridge to pop in the oven first thing in the morning—which makes being thoughtful even easier!

I have been making these cinnamon buns for years, but only in the past few have I started using the shortcut method. While it's fun to make the dough from scratch, it's much more time-consuming and not that easy on your hands (especially if you have arthritis). Using store-bought bread dough as opposed to making your own makes these super-easy for anyone to turn out these supremely impressive cinnamon rolls.

If you have a loved one who is a devotee of the cinnamon rolls in the mall, expect them to become your number one fan the moment these come out of the oven. Of course, since I do have two ways of making these, I'm going to give you my easy way and then my homemade dough recipe just in case any of you want to try out that method as well. I'll stick with my shortcut method though—life is complicated enough.

filling

1 loaf frozen white bread dough (such as Rhode's)

4 tablespoons (½ stick) butter or margarine, softened

Preheat the oven to 400°F and grease a 9 x 13-inch baking pan.

Place the loaf of dough on a plate and let sit at room temperature until thawed. Once thawed, roll out onto a floured surface to a size of about 9 by 16 inches. Spread 4 tablespoons butter over the dough.

1 cup packed brown sugar

3 tablespoons ground cinnamon

In a small bowl, mix together the brown sugar and cinnamon. Sprinkle over the top of the cinnamon roll, stopping about ½ inch away from the sides so it will seal. Carefully roll up the cinnamon roll into a log and press lightly to seal. Cut into 1-inch slices with a serrated knife.

Place in the baking pan and cover with plastic wrap. Place in a warm spot and allow to rise until doubled in size. Remove the plastic wrap and bake for about 15 minutes, until done, lightly browned on top.

icing

3 ounces cream cheese, softened

4 tablespoons (½ stick) butter or margarine, softened

1½ cups confectioners' sugar

½ teaspoon vanilla extract, optional (I usually just leave it out)

To make the icing, mix all the icing ingredients together and beat with an electric mixer until creamy. Spread over the warm cinnamon rolls.

16 rolls

cinnamon buns
with dough from scratch

this dough replaces the frozen loaf of bread dough in the previous recipe. Use the rest of the recipe as written on page 194.

1 cup lukewarm milk

2 large eggs, at room temperature

⅓ cup unsalted butter or margarine, cut up

4¾ cups all-purpose flour

1¾ teaspoons salt

½ cup sugar

2½ teaspoons instant or bread machine yeast

Place all of the dough ingredients into the pan of your bread machine in the order listed. Program the machine for dough or manual and press start. After about 10 minutes, check the consistency of the dough. It should be smooth, not too sticky, and not too dry. Adjust its consistency with additional flour or water if necessary to allow the machine to complete the kneading.

If you're not using a bread machine, combine all of the dough ingredients in a large bowl and stir until the mixture becomes cohesive. Transfer to a lightly oiled work surface and knead by hand for 5 to 8 minutes, or until it is smooth. The way I think of smooth is that it needs to be like a baby's bottom.

Place the kneaded dough in a lightly oiled bowl and turn to grease all sides. Cover the bowl with plastic wrap and let rise in a warm place for 1 hour, or until it is nearly doubled in size. Transfer to a floured work surface and roll into a 16 x 21-inch rectangle. Complete using the recipe on page 194.

32 rolls

lucille's potato salad

I was never a fan of potato salad until I tried my grandmother Lucille's, and I've heard other folks say the same thing. This is a good old-fashioned recipe that's as Southern as the day is long.

Note from Grandmother Lucille: Potato salad varies in how thick it turns out. If it is too thick after mixing, you can add a little pickle juice or extra mayonnaise to make it the right consistency for your taste.

3 cups peeled, cubed, and cooked potatoes

3 eggs, hard-boiled and chopped

½ cup mayonnaise

2 tablespoons yellow mustard

One 4-ounce jar diced pimento, drained

⅓ cup sweet relish or diced sweet pickles

¼ cup finely diced onion

Salt and pepper to taste

In a large bowl, combine all the ingredients and stir well. Serve warm or refrigerate and serve cold.

8 servings

baked macaroni and cheese

macaroni and cheese is a must-have whenever kids are around, and there are countless takes on this classic comfort food, so I couldn't bring you just one. This is the recipe for the baked version, which is for those who prefer stringy, extra cheesy mac and cheese. It's best made in an ovenproof bowl rather than a 9 x 13-inch pan.

2½ **cups uncooked macaroni**

2½ **tablespoons all-purpose flour**

1¼ **teaspoons salt**

Black pepper to taste (I use about 1 teaspoon)

4 **tablespoons (½ stick) margarine, cut into small slices**

3 **cups shredded cheddar cheese**

1 **cup milk**

Preheat the oven to 350°F.

Cook the pasta according to the package directions until tender and drain. In a large bowl, combine the flour, salt, and pepper and set aside. Spray an oven-safe bowl or dish with cooking spray. Place half of the macaroni in the bowl or dish. Sprinkle half of the flour mixture over the top and then top with half of the margarine slices. Sprinkle 1½ cups of the cheese over the top. Repeat. Pour the milk over all. Cover with foil and bake for 35 minutes. Remove the foil and bake for an additional 10 minutes, until bubbly. Serve hot.

8 servings

creamy macaroni and cheese

this is my mother's smooth and creamy macaroni and cheese recipe and the one that all of the kids love best. Just remember that everything here comes in twos, it's that easy!

2 cups dry macaroni

2 tablespoons margarine

2 tablespoons all-purpose flour

2 cups whole milk

Salt and black pepper to taste

2 cups cubed Velveeta

Preheat the oven to 350°F.

Cook the macaroni according to the package directions until almost done and drain well.

In a microwave-safe bowl, melt the margarine in the microwave. Stir in the flour, then the milk. Season with salt and pepper. Pour the cubed cheese into the milk mixture and microwave at 30-second intervals until melted, stirring each time you check it. Stir in the cooked macaroni. Place in an oven-safe dish and bake, uncovered, for 20 minutes, or until bubbly.

8 servings

chicken poulet

I always laugh when Mama talks about this recipe because the name translates to "chicken chicken." This dish is really pretty convenient because you can assemble it the night before and just stick it in your refrigerator. Come home from work or a day of running the errand rat race and top it with your cream soup, pop it in the oven, and supper is on its way!

½ cup (1 stick) margarine

1 cup water

One 16-ounce package Pepperidge Farm cornbread stuffing mix

4 eggs

2 cups chicken broth

2 chicken breasts, cooked and shredded

½ cup mayonnaise

¼ cup chopped green onions

Sprinkling of salt

1 cup milk

One 10.5-ounce can cream of mushroom soup, undiluted

1 cup shredded cheddar cheese

Combine the margarine and water in a microwave-safe bowl and melt the margarine in the microwave.

Place the stuffing mix in a large bowl. Pour the water and margarine mixture over it and stir. Add 2 of the eggs and the chicken broth and stir to combine.

In a separate bowl, combine the shredded chicken, mayonnaise, and green onions. Stir well.

Place half of the stuffing mix in the bottom of a 9 x 13-inch pan. Top with all of the chicken mixture. Sprinkle with salt. Top with the remaining stuffing mix. Beat together the remaining 2 eggs and the milk. Pour over the mixture in the pan—the mixture will look soupy. Cover and refrigerate for at least 8 hours, or you can make it the night before and bake it at suppertime the following day.

Preheat the oven to 350°F.

Before baking, remove the cover and spread the cream of mushroom soup over the top. Place in the oven and bake, uncovered, for 45 minutes. Remove from the oven and top with the shredded cheese. Return to the oven for another 5 minutes, or until the cheese is melted.

8 to 10 servings

kathy's country casserole

in my family, if you die, get sick, have a car accident, have a baby, have a potluck, family reunion, or picnic, get bad news, get hungry, or get last-minute dinner guests . . . you get a country casserole!

This casserole freezes well and can be made even more convenient by using canned chicken. If you have a vegetarian in the family, substitute the cream of chicken soup with cream of celery, double the vegetables, and leave out the chicken.

2 cups small shell pasta, cooked and drained

2 cups frozen mixed vegetables, cooked and drained

2 cups shredded cheddar cheese

1 cup french-fried onions

2 cups shredded cooked chicken (you can use canned chicken)

One 10.5-can cream of chicken soup, undiluted

½ cup milk

1 teaspoon black pepper

¼ teaspoon garlic powder

½ teaspoon salt

Preheat the oven to 350°F.

Combine everything in a large bowl, reserving half of the cheese and half of the french-fried onions for topping later.

Spoon into a 9 x 13-inch casserole dish. Bake for 25 minutes. Top with the remaining french-fried onions and cheese and bake until the cheese is melted, about 5 minutes more.

Freezing options: Instead of freezing this in your casserole dish, simply spoon it into a gallon zipper-seal bag. Lay the bag flat so it will thaw out quicker and place it in your freezer. Take it out the night before the day you want it and refrigerate or place in the fridge that morning.

If you forget to do all of this, no sweat! Just microwave the bag until it thaws just a bit, pour into your casserole, and bake.

To bake a casserole that is still frozen, simply place in the oven while the oven preheats. This allows the casserole to thaw quickly and then bake to perfection.

8 servings

eye of round roast

this was often part of our Sunday dinner fare, and I still love it to this day. The recipe in and of itself is as simple as it can be, but the resulting flavor of the meat is out of this world. I suggest using an electric knife to cut thin slices and serving alongside MeMe's Mashed Potatoes (page 35).

Cracked or coarsely ground pepper

Eye of round roast

Preheat the oven to 500°F.

Generously pepper the roast. Place in a pan lined with aluminum foil or sprayed with cooking spray. Place the roast in the oven and bake for 5 minutes per pound plus 10 minutes. Turn off the oven—DO NOT OPEN THE OVEN for 2 hours. If it is a long eye of round, cut in half and place side by side in a pan, leaving a little space between the halves.

6 to 8 servings

grandma lucy's pimento cheese

long before the days of snack cakes and convenience foods, pimento cheese sandwiches dominated minds when it came to a "quick bite to eat" or a "little lunch." They were cheap and delicious on plain old white bread, although I serve mine on wheat these days.

I remember going to Grandmama and Granddaddy's house and finding one or both sitting at their kitchen table having a pimento cheese sandwich and a glass of milk. They'd always ask, "Ya want some puh-men-ah cheese, baby?" I never refused.

One 16-ounce block Velveeta, at room temperature

One 2-ounce jar pimentos, drained

½ **cup mayonnaise**

Salt and pepper to taste, optional

Push the Velveeta through a grater into a bowl until all is grated. Add the pimentos and mayonnaise. Stir well. Season with salt and pepper, if desired. Serve on loaf bread.

2 cups

bologna as a judge of character

when my mama was a girl, her family had a tradition of going out riding through the countryside on Sunday afternoons. They'd stop off at a little store to have thick slices of bologna cut off and made into bologna and cheese sandwiches. Pair that with a bottled drink and they were living high on the hog. "There just wasn't anything like getting to ride in that car and looking out the window while you ate a bologna sandwich!"

This treat was passed down to my generation: We would often sit down for lunch with a big loaf of bread and a stack of cheese slices in the middle of the table while Mama fried up bologna in a skillet. We'd each make our own sandwich and I'd make mine just like my brother did: fried bologna, cheese, and potato chips settled in between two pieces of "loaf bread."

Bologna sandwiches, sometimes referred to as "the poor man's steak," are such a big part of our culture that they're even used to gauge a person's character. On the day we got married, my husband's best man, Jim, had driven in a ways and was planning on staying overnight before heading back home. He stayed with my grandmother, who lived across the road from what was to be our new home. It had been quite a day with the wedding and reception, and that evening Grandmama and Jim went out on her porch to relax and look out over the river.

For supper, Grandmama made the two of them bologna sandwiches.

To Grandmama, Jim and my husband represented a new generation, with a huge divide between folks her age. Grandmama had grown up dirt poor, picking cotton all of her life, and here was this young man newly graduated from college with an engineering degree whose experience in her world had been nothing more than glancing at the cotton as the car went by. Sometimes it's a little intimidating for folks who come from such humble backgrounds to be in situations like this, but when Jim accepted that bologna sandwich, it spoke volumes to Grandmama about the type of person he was at heart. Even now, whenever he is mentioned she always chimes in, "Jim is just a real good boy, he sat out there on the porch and ate a bologna sandwich with me."

To fry bologna, simply place a slice in a skillet and cook over medium heat until it is browned on both sides, although I prefer mine black!

granny jordan's chicken salad

Granny Jordan used to make this chicken salad recipe for her ladies' group at church, and in the South there is no finer food than what is served at a church luncheon. You'll find it delicious served hot, but if there is any left over, it's just as good served cold over crackers as well. We have tried to figure out which way we like best and are never able to decide. I think we need to make this a few hundred more times and then we'll make up our minds.

1 **cooked chicken, cut up**

½ **cup mayonnaise**

One 10.5-ounce can cream of
   chicken soup, undiluted

2 **hard-boiled eggs, cut up**

¾ **cup diced celery**

½ **onion, diced**

⅓ **cup cracker crumbs,**
   optional

   Potato chips

   Lettuce, optional

   Ritz crackers, optional

Preheat the oven to 350°F. Mix the chicken, mayonnaise, soup, eggs, celery, onion, and cracker crumbs in a bowl. Spread into an 8 x 8-inch pan. Top with crushed potato chips. Bake for 20 minutes. Serve hot or cold. If serving cold, serve over a bed of lettuce with Ritz crackers.

6 servings

*The Beauty of
Grandmothers*

The real beauty behind a Southern granny is that you can spend all day at her house, from sunup till sundown, yapping and eating and laughing and carrying on, then when you finally get ready to go, even if it's ten hours later, she'll look at you with a pained expression and say with her heart in her throat, "Awww, y'all . . . please don't rush off."

daddy's rise-and-shine biscuits

biscuits are such a staple of the Southern diet that it's usually one of the first things folks think about when they think of Southern food. Back in the day, folks bought flour in twenty-five-pound sacks, so biscuits and dumplings and such were a great way to make a meager meal more filling for the whole family. Oftentimes, meals consisted of biscuits and a little milk gravy, made using some bacon grease for seasoning. This was a completely meatless meal that still managed to fill stomachs before setting off to a hard day's work. My great-aunt Louise often said, "Many a family would have starved if not for biscuits and gravy." This is one of many reasons why biscuits still hold a revered place at Southern dinner tables. Still, a lot of folks end up disappointed in their biscuits, as they turn out flat and tough. This method of preparation helps to ensure there is no overkneading. People who've never been able to make a light and fluffy biscuit have reported back that theirs turned out beautiful after trying this recipe.

2¼ cups self-rising flour (see Note)

½ cup (1 stick) butter or margarine, softened

1¼ cups buttermilk (see page 265 for how to make your own)

All-purpose flour for dusting

Melted butter for brushing the baked biscuits

Preheat the oven to 450°F and grease a baking sheet.

Place the flour in a large bowl. Cut the butter in with a long-tined fork until crumbly. Cover and place in the refrigerator for 10 minutes. Slowly pour in the buttermilk and stir just until moistened.

Turn the dough out onto a floured surface and knead three or four times with your hands, adding flour as needed to prevent sticking. With well-floured hands, pat the dough out into a rectangle about ¾ inch thick. Fold each side over into the center as if folding a letter. Repeat two more times, beginning with patting the dough out.

Pat the dough out a final time until it is ½ inch thick. Cut with a biscuit cutter dipped in flour and place the biscuits on the baking sheet with the sides touching. Bake for 12 to 15 minutes, until lightly browned. Remove from the oven and brush the tops with melted butter.

Note: To make your own self-rising flour, simply add 1½ teaspoons baking powder and ½ teaspoon salt for each cup of all-purpose flour.

10 to 12 biscuits

basic milk gravy

gravy is practically a food group where I'm from. When folks didn't have much to offer but biscuits as a meal, gravy was a means of making the meal more filling and rounding it out a bit.

The following gravies are traditionally served over biscuits but are also great served over meatloaf, hamburger steaks, or even a simple slice of bread.

milk gravy

- **3 tablespoons bacon grease or oil**
- **¼ cup all-purpose flour**
- **½ teaspoon salt**
- **¼ teaspoon black pepper**
- **1½ cups milk**

Pour the bacon grease into a medium skillet and heat over medium heat. Add the flour and stir to combine. Add the salt and pepper. Cook, stirring constantly, until the flour begins to brown. Slowly pour in the milk, stirring constantly with a wire whisk to break up any lumps. Lower the heat to low and continue cooking and stirring until the gravy thickens. This will happen pretty fast, so stay on your toes! If you prefer a thinner gravy, add more milk.

sausage gravy

- **¼ pound sausage**
- **¼ cup all-purpose flour**
- **½ teaspoon salt**
- **¼ teaspoon black pepper**
- **1½ cups milk**

Brown the sausage in a medium skillet over medium heat. Remove from the skillet and crumble it. Return the sausage to the skillet and stir the flour into the sausage and sausage grease. Add the salt and pepper. Cook, stirring constantly, until the flour begins to brown. Slowly pour in the milk, stirring constantly with a wire whisk to break up any lumps. Lower the heat to low and continue cooking and stirring until the gravy thickens. This will happen pretty fast, so stay on your toes! If you prefer a thinner gravy, add more milk.

6 servings

tomato gravy

- **3 tablespoons bacon grease or oil**
- **¼ cup all-purpose flour**
- **½ teaspoon salt**
- **¼ teaspoon black pepper**
- **1½ cups milk**
- **One 15-ounce can diced tomatoes, drained**

Pour the bacon grease into a medium skillet and heat over medium heat. Add the flour and stir to combine. Add the salt and pepper. Cook, stirring constantly, until the flour begins to brown. Slowly pour in the milk, stirring constantly with a wire whisk to break up any lumps. Lower the heat to low and continue cooking and stirring until the gravy thickens. This will happen pretty fast, so stay on your toes! Add the diced tomatoes. Lightly mash the tomatoes with a fork to break them up into smaller pieces and stir until heated through. Don't mind the lumps from the tomatoes—that's what gives tomato gravy its character.

red-eye gravy

- **2 tablespoons vegetable oil**
- **1 slice country ham (see Note)**
- **1 teaspoon sugar**
- **⅔ cup hot coffee**

Pour the oil into a medium skillet and heat over medium heat. Add the ham and cook until lightly browned or both sides. Remove the ham to a plate. Pour the grease off into a small bowl. Sprinkle the sugar over the hot skillet. When the sugar begins to bubble and brown, pour the hot coffee into the skillet. Swirl around inside the skillet until it begins to boil, and then pour over the reserved grease. To serve, dip from the bottom of the bowl to get the "red eye."

Note: You can make as much or as little country ham as you want, but you need at least one slice to leave the flavor in the skillet, which is the base of red-eye gravy.

chocolate gravy

in days of old, with flour in abundance and other resources scarce, biscuits made a great breakfast and filling snack any time of day. Eating sweets was not a regular occurrence, and so waking up in the morning to find fresh biscuits and a boat of chocolate gravy was a wondrous treat. It was poured over the buttered biscuits, then the tender bread would soak it up, transforming the biscuit into a decadently saturated little chocolate cake.

Outside of the South, chocolate gravy is unheard of, and I've gotten many a horrified look when I've mentioned it to friends from other areas. But it's a Southern classic if there ever was one—it should be in the hall of honor right there with the chicken and dumplings and biscuits. Here is my recipe—don't try it unless you want the flavor to linger in your mind for the rest of your life.

1 cup sugar or Splenda

2 tablespoons all-purpose flour

1 tablespoon unsweetened cocoa powder

1¼ cups milk

1 tablespoon butter

Combine everything except the butter in a medium heavy saucepan. Bring to a boil over medium heat, stirring constantly to prevent scorching. Reduce the heat and stir for a minute more (it will get pretty thick rather suddenly). Stir in the butter and pour over the biscuits. I tear my biscuit up in a bowl first and then pour it over. You can die happy now.

4 to 6 servings

why life is good right now

for many of us, times are more difficult now than we can remember them ever being. Even if your lifestyle hasn't changed, the impact of others' lives having changed so much is still there. This is something that weighs heavily on my heart because I see so many people filled with worry, yet on the same token, I also see so many positive changes coming about as a result.

You see, sometimes bad things exist only to pave the way for more good things, and these days, I feel that's just what is happening. It's all in your perspective, for the most part.

Maybe we have less. Maybe we eat at home more, as a family around a dinner table filled with something cooked from scratch by someone who loves us. Maybe we have fewer preservatives and red dye #40 and a little more biscuits and milk gravy. Maybe we sit and drink our coffee at the breakfast table instead of in a paper cup handed to us through a drive-through window.

Maybe we buy the kids fewer toys. When I was little I had the best rocket ships, doll cradles, and telephone system around—all made from empty oatmeal canisters. I'd spend hours crafting them, gluing paper on them to cover up the labels, and then designing the new look with crayons. Mama would give me old wash rags to use as blankets, and then she and I would take scraps and sew little pillows by hand for my dolls (or astronauts) to use.

Folks would pay good money for that kind of entertainment for their kids these days, and yet it still sits in the same place it has for generations, on the pantry shelf just waiting to offer up a nutritious breakfast and comfy nap space for dolly.

Sometimes we need to realize that something bad can come along to help us take

our eyes off of something worse, and realize that what we have at the core of things is something really, really good.

I'm not saying we don't appreciate the good things in life or that we've lost our sense of values, just that perhaps now that the glaring, beeping things before us have toned down a bit, in the silence it's not quite so hard to hear when a child whispers your name or to see their expectant smile aimed in your direction.

Still, I hope that everyone gets more money and those without become those with again. Of course, I wish the best for everyone. But chances are, there's something pretty darn good right there with you now. It might even be waiting to curl up in your lap or for you to simply look up and take notice.

All my life I dreamed of having a family. I have two gorgeous, happy, and healthy kids and a husband who loves us all. Just because the price of groceries has gone up doesn't make my dream any less realized.

I don't know if I'm willing to go out on a limb as an authority and state that there is good in everything bad, but I can tell you there has been good in everything I've seen so far.

I may not be eating steak or wearing expensive clothes. I may not drive a fancy car and my bank balance may be woefully lacking in digits, but just take a look at all that I do have in my life—things that money could never buy—and don't you tell me I'm not rich.

mama reed's tea cakes

if you've never had a Southern tea cake, they are rather difficult to describe. I can assure you, though, despite appearances, it is nothing like a cookie. This tender little cake is soft and pillowy, with just a touch of sweetness. A very simple and comforting flavor, they are generally only iced for company or special occasions, at other times getting only a light sprinkling of sugar as they come out of the oven.

This recipe is from my great-grandmother Mama Reed. I never got to know her, but my mother can't help but smile every time she speaks her name.

1 cup (2 sticks) butter or margarine

1 cup granulated sugar, plus more for sprinkling

3 eggs

3½ cups self-rising flour

1 teaspoon vanilla extract

Preheat the oven to 350°F.

In a large bowl, cream the butter and sugar. Add the eggs and mix again. Add the flour and vanilla and mix well. Roll thin on a floured board and cut with a cookie or biscuit cutter. Place on a greased cookie sheet and bake for 10 minutes, until lightly browned on the edges. Sprinkle with sugar while still warm or ice with simple icing (recipe follows), then cool.

simple icing

2 tablespoons butter or margarine, softened

½ cup confectioners' sugar

2 tablespoons milk, plus more if needed

1 teaspoon vanilla extract

A few drops of food coloring

In a large bowl, cut the butter into the confectioners' sugar. Add the milk and stir until any lumps are gone. Add the vanilla and food coloring, and stir until combined. Spoon onto cookies or tea cakes and spread with the back of a spoon. Top with sprinkles while still wet, if desired. Let dry before stacking and storing.

approximately 3 dozen tea cakes

watergate salad

Mama has made this for as long as I can remember, but I shunned it as a child because it "looked weird." I wondered why Mama never complained of my pickiness until my own daughter did the same thing. My immediate thought was, "More for me!"

One 20-ounce can crushed pineapple (juice and all)

1 cup mini marshmallows

1 cup chopped pecans

1 small box instant pistachio pudding (I use sugar-free)

8 ounces whipped topping (you can use light or the reduced-sugar variety)

In a large bowl, mix all the ingredients together well. Chill before serving. If the salad is a little thick, it can be thinned with a bit of milk.

8 servings

Congealed Salads

Aside from fresh-from-the-garden vegetables and iced tea, nothing says summer gathering to a Southerner like congealed salad. However, outside of the southern United States, most folks refer to them as gelatin salads. We just like to be different.

The possibilities of a congealed salad are endless, much to the delight of its devotees. My great-grandmother, who lived the majority of her life as a sharecropper, considered congealed salads to be the ultimate treat. Back in her day, though, it was a treat that could only be enjoyed in the winter because they didn't have a refrigerator. Alabama summers would never allow the gelatin to set up in this heat!

My grandmother says that in the wintertime Lela had an old wash tub she kept out back of her house. She'd let it fill up with water, and as soon as it got cold enough to freeze, off she'd go to mix up a congealed salad in her kitchen and then put it out on top of that ice to set up in time for dinner.

When Lela was older, she lived with my grandmama and granddaddy. Each week they'd make their pilgrimage to the grocery store, the one time Lela went out. She'd get dressed up in her good dress and hard leather shoes, hook her black handbag in the crook of her arm, and come back with twinkling eyes and a brand-new container of premade congealed salad. In her mind, she had really moved up in the world to be able to afford such a thing!

fresh strawberry pie

I love it when my mother makes this pie, because she always doubles the recipe and sends one to my house. Using my quick and easy mix-in-the-pan pie crust, you can throw together this gorgeous pie quick as a wink.

1 cup sugar

3 heaping tablespoons cornstarch

3 tablespoons strawberry gelatin mix

1 cup water

1 pint fresh strawberries, hulled and cut in half

1 pie crust, cooked and cooled (store-bought or mix-in-the-pan crust on page 221)

In a medium saucepan, combine the sugar, cornstarch, and dry gelatin and stir well. Add the water and cook over medium-high heat, until thick and clear, stirring constantly to prevent scorching. Set aside and let cool.

Arrange the strawberries over the pie crust. When the filling has cooled, pour it over the strawberries and chill the pie until ready to serve. Serve with whipped cream, and think of me when you eat a piece.

8 servings

mix-in-the-pan crust

this is one of my basic recipes that has come in handy for me on several occasions. A good old-fashioned no-muss no-fuss mix-in-the-pan pie crust. This is easy-peasy—and doesn't even dirty up a bowl. It works beautifully with good old-fashioned pies.

1½ **cups all-purpose flour**

1 **teaspoon salt**

1½ **teaspoons sugar**

2 **tablespoons milk**

½ **cup cooking oil**

Preheat the oven to 350°F. Mix the flour, salt, and sugar in a pie pan. Slowly add the milk and oil. Mix well with a fork and pat out to fit the pan. Bake until browned, about 10 minutes.

1 pie crust

fried green tomatoes

fried green tomatoes are one of the essential Southern dishes. I can imagine they came about by folks who weathered the winter and were just itching for something fresh from the garden. Add a little flour and cornmeal and a delicacy is born. I often fry one up and eat only that for lunch.

I also fry eggplant the exact same way. The only difference is that you need to slice your eggplant and salt each side. Let the slices sit for a few minutes and then blot the moisture off each side with a paper towel. Proceed with the rest of the recipe as if they were tomato slices.

2 medium green tomatoes
1 cup cornmeal
½ cup all-purpose flour
2 teaspoons seasoned salt
½ cup buttermilk
Oil for frying

Wash and slice the tomatoes. Do not peel them. Mix the cornmeal, flour, and seasoned salt in a gallon bag. Dip the tomato slices in the buttermilk and then place in the bag, a few at a time, to coat with the flour-cornmeal mixture.

Fill a large skillet with approximately ¼ inch of oil. Place over medium-high heat, and when the oil is hot, add a few slices at a time. Fry until browned on one side, then turn and brown on the other side. Drain on a paper towel–lined platter.

4 to 6 servings

Why Southerners Are Seasonal Eaters

By now you've probably noticed that this book isn't laid out like other cookbooks. Rather than arrange it by category, I chose to arrange it by season, our natural way of eating. Ever wonder why Southerners only eat certain dishes at specific times of year? People indigenous to the Old South learned to eat according to season due to lack of refrigeration and a subtropical climate. This manner of eating and these food choices are still followed today out of custom and habit.

fried okra

this is a classic Southern fried okra that utilizes the convenience of store-bought pre-sliced pieces. If you'd rather use fresh, simply slice it and proceed with the recipe. There is nothing quite like fried okra to round out a meal, and despite how much of it I cook, there never seems to be enough.

About 4 cups okra (fresh or frozen), sliced

1 cup cornmeal (self-rising or all-purpose)

1 teaspoon salt

1 teaspoon black pepper

¼ cup vegetable oil

Thaw the okra if using frozen and place in a large bowl. Sprinkle the cornmeal over the okra. Add the salt and pepper. Stir the okra to coat with the cornmeal.

Fill a large skillet with approximately ¼ cup oil. Place over medium-high heat and heat until hot. Using a slotted spoon, dip the okra from the bowl into the oil. (Leave the extra cornmeal in the bowl and throw it away.) Cook until the okra is browned and crisp, stirring occasionally. Remove from the oil with a slotted spoon.

4 to 6 servings

vegetable sandwich spread

these make the loveliest little sandwiches if you're having friends over for iced tea or for a party spread. I also like to serve them at baby showers and bridal showers.

2 envelopes unflavored gelatin

½ cup cold water

1½ cups mayonnaise

1 tablespoon lemon juice

1 package Hidden Valley Ranch Dressing mix

1¾ cups shredded carrots

1 cup finely chopped celery

1 large cucumber, seeded and diced

1 small onion, finely diced

In a medium saucepan, sprinkle the gelatin over the cold water; let stand for 1 minute, then heat over low heat, stirring until blended. Remove from the heat, let cool, and add the mayonnaise, lemon juice, and ranch dressing.

Combine all the vegetables in a large bowl and stir in the dressing. Cover and refrigerate until ready to use. Spread on sandwich bread.

3 cups

green bean and shoepeg corn casserole

here is another one of Granny Jordan's recipes—this was one of her signature dishes that she always brought to Easter dinner. Now my sister-in-law and I carry on the tradition. If you can't find shoepeg corn, you can substitute whole kernel yellow corn instead.

½ **cup chopped onion**

½ **cup chopped celery**

¼ **cup chopped bell pepper**

½ **cup grated sharp cheddar cheese**

One **11-ounce can shoepeg corn, drained**

One **11-ounce can French-style green beans, drained**

One **11-ounce can cream of celery soup, undiluted**

½ **pint sour cream**

½ **cup crushed Ritz crackers**

4 **tablespoons (½ stick) margarine or butter**

Preheat the oven to 350°F.

In a large bowl, mix all the ingredients together except for the crackers and margarine. Place in a casserole dish. Melt the margarine in a skillet and mix with the crushed Ritz crackers. Spread over the top of the vegetables and bake for 45 minutes, or until bubbly.

8 to 10 servings

lemon bars

these are an old family favorite, loved by all, but especially by my grandmother Lucille. Several years back, she was invited to a get-together and mentioned that she needed to take a dish. I told her that I was planning on making lemon bars that day and I'd just make up an extra batch that she could drop by and pick up on her way.

I had no idea that Grandmama had never tasted a lemon bar before. She pulled back the cover to sample one, and I knew by the look on her face after the first bite that we shared our love of these buttery little treats. I asked her that evening how they had been received, and she just started laughing. By the time she got there, she had eaten a few more and ended up liking them so much that she told her host she'd not had time to bake anything, keeping the lemon bars hidden in her car to take back home!

crust

2 cups all-purpose flour

½ cup confectioners' sugar

1 cup (2 sticks) butter or margarine, softened

Preheat the oven to 350°F.

Sift together the flour and confectioners' sugar into a large bowl. Cut in the butter until the mixture sticks together. Press into a 9 x 13-inch dish. Bake for 25 minutes, or until lightly browned. Remove from the oven to cool. Leave the oven on.

filling

4 eggs, beaten

2 cups granulated sugar

⅓ cup lemon juice

½ cup all-purpose flour

½ teaspoon baking powder

¼ cup confectioners' sugar

While the crust is cooling, make the filling. In a large bowl, combine the beaten eggs, granulated sugar, and lemon juice. In a separate bowl, sift the flour and baking powder; stir into the egg mixture. Pour over the baked crust and bake for 15 minutes, or until slightly browned and set. Remove from the oven, cool, and sprinkle with confectioners' sugar. Cut into bars.

12 servings

preston rolls

these rolls were the specialty of the Preston family gatherings. My Aunt Wanda (Mama's stepsister) was a Preston after she married and brought this roll recipe back to our family. Mama said there was nothing like the smell of Preston rolls baking in the oven.

3 packages RapidRise™ yeast

1 cup lukewarm water

1 cup boiling water

1 cup shortening

2 eggs, well beaten

6 cups all-purpose flour, sifted

½ cup sugar

1 teaspoon salt

In a small bowl, dissolve the yeast in the lukewarm water. Set aside.

Pour the boiling water over the shortening in a large bowl. Mix the eggs into the yeast mixture. Pour the yeast and egg mixture into the shortening mixture.

In a separate bowl, sift the flour, sugar, and salt together. Add the dry ingredients to the wet ingredients and mix well with a wooden spoon.

Pour the dough into a well-oiled sealable container and seal. Place in the refrigerator overnight. Punch down the dough before bed and again the next morning. Two hours before serving, take the dough out of the refrigerator and knead a few times on a floured surface. Roll out to a ½-inch thickness and cut out with a round biscuit cutter. Place in a greased pan and let rise for 2 hours.

Preheat the oven to 425°F. Bake for 15 to 20 minutes, or until browned.

2 dozen rolls

thousand island dressing

if you like Thousand Island dressing, here is a warning: Tasting this homemade dressing will officially ruin you for all other versions. This is Thousand Island at its freshest, creamiest best.

We eat this on hamburgers and salads, dip carrots and celery sticks in it, and I have been known to go to the fridge with a spoon from time to time just to taste it!

1 quart mayonnaise

4 hard-boiled eggs, chopped

7 ounces chili sauce

4 ounces pickle relish

1 teaspoon minced onion

2½ ounces finely chopped pimento

In a bowl, mix all the ingredients well and refrigerate overnight (you may add a little milk if you want yours to be thinner).

2 quarts

collard greens with pepper sauce

I have always loved greens. Turnip, collard, or mixed, I just adore them. Among my favorite recipes for greens, my grandmama's ranks the absolute highest. No one can make them like her. However, I did learn that there is such a thing as too much of a good thing.

When I was working on my Home Economics degree, I lived with my grandparents for a while. Granddaddy passed away while I was living there, and then it was just Grandmama and me. You can imagine how very different life was for the both of us with Granddaddy gone. Being a Southern lady, Grandmama needed someone to take care of—because that's just what Southern women do. I had mentioned before how much I enjoyed Grandmama's greens, and she was off to the races with a cause.

Every day for lunch, we had turnip greens. Every day for supper, we had turnip greens. There might have been a day or two in there when we had them only once, but they always made an appearance before the sun went down, carried to the table by a very pleased-looking Grandmama as she bragged about how much I loved to eat them. I ate every bite, every day, at every meal she served them at. After a month or two, I half expected to look in the mirror and find my skin had turned green.

I laugh now, just as I did then, about Grandmama making me greens so much. I did get a little weary after a while, but the thought that was behind them still made them delicious, and to this day I still count them among some of my favorite dishes.

Greens are an essential part of our New Year's Day meal in the South. According to our tradition, the amount of greens you eat is directly proportionate to how much money you will have in the coming year. Even my brother, who has picky eating habits that rival the most obstinate toddler, has been known to manage a bite or two on New Year's Day.

3 bunches collard greens

¾ cup cider vinegar

2 quarts water

¼ cup salt

1 tablespoon sugar

A ham hock, ham bone, or pieces of country ham, optional

Rinse the greens well. Remove the spines, coarsely chop, and place in a pot. Add all the other ingredients and bring to a boil. Reduce the heat and simmer until the collards are tender, about 2 hours, adding more water if needed. Serve warm with hot pepper sauce (recipe follows).

6 to 8 servings

hot pepper sauce

- 3 cups water
- 1 cup white vinegar
- 1 tablespoon sugar
- 1 tablespoon salt
- 4 whole hot jarred peppers
- 1 teaspoon minced garlic

Combine all the ingredients in a large saucepan and bring to a boil. Reduce the heat and simmer until reduced by half, 30 to 45 minutes. Drizzle over greens or other vegetables. Refrigerate any remaining sauce.

family
favorites

· · · · ·

everybody deserves to be someone's favorite. I had thirteen living grandparents when I was born and I knew each and every one of them. They were special people, each unique in their own way. Some were more inclined to grandparenting than others, but even with the ones who weren't, I still had quite an abundance on my hands.

I had countless opportunities to spend time with my grandparents, to listen and to learn whatever they were willing to teach or pass down. I wouldn't be human, though, if I didn't consider some just a little more special than others.

My granddaddy JM was one such person. JM Pockrus didn't actually have a first name. For some reason, when he was born, his mother simply gave him the initials J and M. Folks who knew him called him "Jay," but some misunderstood the spelling and added an "i" in between, calling him "Jim." Though he was my step-grandfather, he and my grandmother were married when my mother was a teenager, so for me, he was there all along. He was more of a granddaddy to me than anyone could have ever hoped for.

I was also my granddaddy's first granddaughter. All of his life, he'd loved babies and children. He was one of those people (like many of my grandparents) who just had a natural way with kids. Kids knew it, too. They were attracted to this tall, lanky man with the funny haircut who could do a thousand silly faces and would stick his dentures out on demand to make them bounce up and down. I was no different. It had been love at first sight between us, and Granddaddy instantly took me into his heart. Eighteen months later, when my sister was born, he made a declaration to the family that I hadn't got to be the baby long enough and he set out then and there to make it up to me. I was going to be his baby—his favorite.

It seems the rest of his life, whenever we were together, I was at his side. I never sat beside him on the couch or across the room—I sat right up against him, in the crook of his arm, with his arm wrapped around me. I can still feel the warmth of him through his thin cotton shirt and smell the tobacco in the pipe he extinguished whenever I arrived. There was a little table beside him where a stack of crossword puzzles sat. Freshly sharpened pencils filled a tin can, and one or two mason jars filled with circus peanut candy or candy corn sat on the table. My granddaddy smelled like tobacco, pencil lead, and something wonderful.

We used to steal away unnoticed and pick his fig tree clean, eating the figs as we went along and coming back inside empty-handed and grinning. He'd show me his muscles when I asked, me giggling as what appeared to be a softball popped up on his scrawny arm.

We didn't talk much about his childhood or his life—Granddaddy always focused on me. And I, in my childish bliss, thought that was the most important thing of all.

My last memory of Granddaddy was when I was living with him and Grandmama while attending college at The University of North Alabama. I lived downstairs in their lake house and they lived up top. Granddaddy and I had been watching TV together, his arm around me as it had been for well over twenty years. I got up and walked around behind him toward the stairs, leaning down and wrapping my arms around his neck as I kissed the top of his head. Granddaddy reached up and patted my arm. "Love you, babe." "I love you too, Granddaddy."

The next morning he and Grandmama left for a quick trip to Tunica. When they came back, Granddaddy went straight to the hospital. The entire family went to sit vigil at his side, but he had already begun slipping away. I didn't go. I stayed in their house, sitting in his spot on the couch, smelling the tobacco and pencil lead and feeling his warmth, as I'd done so many times before.

I didn't go to Granddaddy's funeral, either. I think most people understood. Some might think that shows a lack of caring, but it wasn't because I didn't love Granddaddy. It was because I loved him too much.

My last memory will always be that night, our last conversation:

"I love you, babe."

"I love you too, Granddaddy."

I wonder if he knows that he was always my favorite, too.

family favorite recipes

aunt louise's beef stew

my great-aunt Louise had curly hair and eyes that lit up when she smiled. She loved kids, and we loved her right back, flocking to her whenever she was visiting.

She was one of those people who had a way of looking as if she were about to impart a joke at any moment, her lips slightly curved up into a secret smile. She always came down to our level when talking to us and had a way of making us feel as if we were in cahoots together against the world, with Louise in our corner.

After being diagnosed with cancer, her first statement to the doctor was, "If I'm gonna die, I don't wanna know." To which the doctor responded, "Well, you are."

Despite that doctor so flippantly setting out to remove the wind from Louise's sails, her spirit would not be dampened. Rather than feel sorry for herself or take to her bed (as any of us would be tempted to do in her place), Louise decided that she wanted to do one more thing for all of us before she left.

With that in mind, she set about crocheting with wild abandon, making a doily for each and every member of her family, right down to me, her great-niece.

I'll never forget the image of her, racing against time as she sat with a scarf tied around her head, bent over her handiwork as she tried to finish each of the doilies.

Aunt Louise left us in 1996, and she finished each doily she had set out to make. Eight years later I had a little girl with curly hair and eyes that light up when she smiles.

These days, Mama and I find ourselves on the phone talking about Louise every time we make her delicious beef stew. "Louise always made the best beef stew. She used those little pearl onions," Mama will say, as if pearl onions are something rich and extravagant. I guess compared to plain old diced ones they are. But after telling you the story of my great-aunt Louise, I'm sure you know that's not the real reason why we enjoy this stew so much—this was her favorite.

6 tablespoons shortening

3 pounds beef stew meat, (cut into 1½-inch cubes)

2 medium onions, coarsely chopped

5 cups water

3 beef bouillon cubes

1 clove garlic, finely chopped

1 teaspoon dried parsley

1 bay leaf

½ teaspoon dried thyme

1½ tablespoons salt

¼ teaspoon black pepper

6 medium potatoes

6 medium carrots

3 stalks celery

10 pearl onions

One 15-ounce can diced tomatoes

Heat the shortening in a Dutch oven over medium heat. Add the beef and brown it well, turning on all sides. Remove from the pot and set aside.

In the same Dutch oven, add the chopped onions and sauté until tender. Return the meat to the pan, add the water, bouillon cubes, garlic, parsley, bay leaf, thyme, salt, and pepper. Cover and simmer until just tender, about 30 minutes.

Cut the potatoes and carrots in chunks and the celery into 3-inch sections.

When the meat is tender, add the potatoes, carrots, pearl onions, and celery. Cook for 1 hour, or until the vegetables are tender, adding the tomatoes 20 minutes before the end of cooking. Serve with crackers or cornbread.

8 servings

chicken and dumplings

many of our most beloved dishes came out of having too little of one thing and a little more of another, and having to stretch it all out to feed a large family. Chicken and dumplings is the perfect example of this.

Back in the day, chicken was a treat and not something offered or even available on a regular basis. Whenever it was, the chicken more often than not was on the scrawny side.

So you have this woman who has a house full of kids to feed and likely a few additional guests after word has gotten out that chicken is on the menu, and only one scrawny little chicken. This is where flour comes to the rescue yet again. Flour could easily be used to stretch a meager meal by making biscuits, dumplings, hoe cake, or an assortment of other improvisational breads and meal stretchers so that an entire family would leave the table feeling full and satisfied.

Today my mother's recipe uses a simpler method but is every bit as good as her grandmother's was.

3 or 4 chicken breasts

32 ounces chicken broth (feel free to substitute water with bouillon cubes added)

One 10.5-ounce can cream of chicken soup

Salt and pepper to taste

One 10-count can layer biscuits

All-purpose flour

Cook the chicken breasts in approximately 4 cups of water until fork-tender, about 45 minutes. Place the broth in a medium to large pot and bring to a gentle boil. Stir the cream of chicken soup into the broth. Tear up the chicken and add it to the broth mixture. Add salt and pepper to taste. Pull the biscuits apart into three layers. Dip each layer into flour and then tear each layer into three pieces and drop into the gently boiling broth mixture. Do not stir the biscuits a lot, or they will cook up—only gently push the dumplings down into the broth as they float to the top. Cook for about 10 minutes after the last dumplings are added. Add the shredded chicken and keep on low heat until ready to serve. The dumplings will become somewhat firm when they are done. If they're gooey, cook 5 to 10 minutes longer.

8 servings

german chocolate pie

my father did not have an easy start in this world. His family was very poor growing up and the true stories of his childhood seem so unrealistic to my kids that I fear they think we're making them up. He rose above it all, though, and even he will tell you that his success in life is due in large part to my mother. They began dating when Mama was only fourteen. By the time Mama was seventeen, Daddy had dropped out of high school and asked her to marry him. She responded, "My daddy won't let me marry anyone who hasn't finished high school," and back he went!

They were married in 1969. Daddy worked as many as three or four jobs at a time when we were little in order to provide for us and make sure Mama could stay home for our benefit.

For my mama, and for most of us, cooking isn't just something on our to-do list each day. It's something we do out of love. Where some folks might bring flowers or buy gifts, we put a gift on the table at each meal, taking care to prepare foods just right for our families.

Daddy is retired now from a successful career in law enforcement. Mama still enjoys cooking for him, though, and this pie is a special one that she makes just for him. Between my parents, I honestly don't know who is the most appreciative, Daddy that he has Mama, or Mama that she has him. We all enjoy the rich chocolate pie, though!

One 4-ounce package German
chocolate

4 tablespoons (½ stick)
margarine

One 12-ounce can evaporated
milk

1½ cups sugar

3 tablespoons cornstarch

⅛ teaspoon salt

2 eggs, lightly beaten

1 teaspoon vanilla extract

1 unbaked deep-dish pie
shell

½ cup chopped pecans

1⅓ cups sweetened flaked
coconut

Preheat the oven to 375°F.

In a small saucepan, melt the chocolate and margarine over low heat, stirring to mix well. Remove from the heat and blend in the evaporated milk. Set aside.

In a large bowl, combine the sugar, cornstarch, and salt. Stir in the eggs and vanilla. Gradually stir in the chocolate mixture. Pour into the pie crust. Combine the pecans and coconut and sprinkle over the filling. Bake for 45 to 50 minutes, until puffed and browned. Cool for about 30 minutes before serving. Refrigerate any leftovers and serve reheated or cold.

8 servings

peach crisp

this recipe is very close to my heart. When I was a little girl, Mama always let me make it. I have memories as early as four years old sitting at the table and stirring the brown sugar into the flour and other ingredients. Of course, Mama did all of the real work, but it takes so little for a child to own a dish. She'd let me stir up the topping and sprinkle it on the peaches, and then she'd place it in the oven. Come suppertime everyone made a grand to do about "Christy's peach crisp" and Mama and Daddy always swore it was the best crisp they'd ever had.

I started my children out making their own peach crisps at a young age, too. I feel it is so very important to get our kids in the kitchen with us when we cook. Not only are you passing on a living and tactile family history, but you're creating memories they'll always cherish. You're also raising their self-esteem, giving them a sense of accomplishment, and teaching skills they'll use for the rest of their lives.

Cooking with your children and grandchildren presents the perfect opportunity to tell them the stories of your childhood and to pass on your values and outlook on life. In today's fast-paced world, people are once again realizing the value of family time around the dinner table, but the real opportunity for making memories begins in the kitchen.

One 29-ounce can sliced peaches, drained

½ cup flour (all-purpose or self-rising)

¾ cup brown sugar

½ cup oats (quick-cooking or old-fashioned)

1 teaspoon ground cinnamon

½ cup (1 stick) margarine or butter, softened

Preheat the oven to 400°F.

Arrange the peach slices in an 8 x 8-inch square pan.

In a large bowl, mix the flour, brown sugar, oats, cinnamon, and margarine with a fork; sprinkle over the peaches.

Bake until lightly browned, about 20 minutes. Serve warm with ice cream.

6 servings

mama reed's baked rice pudding

"always set your table like the president is coming to dinner." That was Mama Reed's philosophy. A kind and generous mother of ten and my great-grandmother, I've only known her through family stories.

My mother used to live next door to her when she was a child. She and her sister would find out what their mother was having for dinner and what Mama Reed was making and then choose which house they wanted to eat at. Mama said they would choose Mama Reed's house quite often. True to her own words, at each and every meal her humble table was set to the nines with all of her Depression glass dinnerware, strategically placed worn silverware, and pressed glass tea glasses that had been originally purchased with peanut butter in them. They may not have had much, but they were proud and willing to share what they did have.

Mama told me a story about the Jewel Tea man coming by one evening, right around suppertime. Of course, Mama Reed invited him to eat, but he had already eaten, so she asked if he'd like a glass of tea. When he said he would, she realized that with a table full of guests already, she had poured out all of the tea and there was none left. Without a thought, she seated him in the living room and walked through the dining room toward the kitchen, grabbing up her untouched glass of tea on her way. In the kitchen, she took an empty glass and put a few ice cubes in it so it would sound as if she were making a new glass. She then appeared with her glass, gave it to him, and later poured a glass of water for herself. That's Southern hospitality.

Of course, Mama Reed was an amazing cook. This is her special recipe for rice pudding and my mother's favorite heartwarming treat. Like the other matriarchs in my family, she was adept at making do with what ingredients were on hand and affordable, which made rice a regular ingredient for her cooking (even now, we all love a bowl of hot rice served with butter and sugar for breakfast). Most rice puddings are cooked in a pot on top of the stove, but our family has always baked rice pudding. When it's baked, it develops a wonderful custard and transforms into a rich and comforting dessert. This pudding would be served for dessert after dinner and any leftovers could be served for breakfast. True comfort food. I'm sure Mama Reed would be proud to know we're still enjoying it today.

4 eggs, beaten

1 cup sugar or Splenda

3 cups milk

½ teaspoon salt

2 teaspoons vanilla extract

2 cups cooked rice

½ teaspoon ground cinnamon

½ cup raisins

Preheat the oven to 300°F and spray an ovenproof casserole dish with cooking spray.

In a large bowl, beat the eggs. Stir in the sugar. Add the other ingredients and stir. Pour the mixture into the casserole dish, set the dish in a pan of hot water, and bake for 30 minutes. Remove from the oven, insert a spoon at the edge of the pudding, and stir from the bottom to distribute the rice and raisins. Return the pudding to the oven and bake for an additional 60 minutes, until set. Serve warm. Leftovers may be eaten hot or cold.

8 servings

mud hens

I just love old Southern recipes with funny names. Mud hens is a classic example. I wish I had some interesting story to tell you about how they got their name, but I honestly haven't a clue; that is just what they are called. Until you've had a mud hen, you can't possibly imagine how gooey and delicious they are, and once you've had one, you'll stop giving strange looks when you hear the name and instead just light up in hopes of being offered one.

Mud hens are made with chocolate chip cookie dough on the bottom, and melted marshmallows and a deliciously delicate brown sugar meringue on top. It's best if you allow them to cool before cutting, but I suggest you sneak one out while still warm because they'll disappear fast. My kids love these as a surprise treat. Chocolate chip cookie lovers will be over the moon!

¼ cup shortening

4 tablespoons (½ stick) butter, at room temperature

1 cup granulated sugar

1 whole egg

2 eggs, separated

1½ cups all-purpose flour

1 teaspoon baking powder

¼ teaspoon salt

1 cup chopped nuts

1 cup mini marshmallows

½ cup Nestle Toll House Semi-Sweet Chocolate Morsels

1 cup packed light brown sugar

Preheat the oven to 350°F and butter a 9 x 13-inch baking pan.

In a large bowl, cream the shortening, butter, and sugar. Beat in the whole egg and 2 egg yolks.

In a separate bowl, sift the flour, baking powder, and salt together. Combine the flour mixture with the creamed mixture, blending thoroughly.

Spread the batter into the baking pan. Sprinkle the nuts, marshmallows, and chocolate chips over the batter.

In a large bowl, beat the 2 egg whites until stiff; fold in the brown sugar and spread over the top of the batter. Bake for 30 to 40 minutes, until lightly browned on top. Cool completely, then cut into bars.

12 servings

slow-cooked pork roast

when we first got married, my husband and I lived in Rogersville, Alabama, while I finished up my degree. Those were a happy few years with my mother living across the street and my grandmother two doors down. We often took turns eating at different houses. Mama cooked some, and one night a week my grandmother Lucille would cook. Nothing got my husband hightailing it home faster than hearing that Grandmama had her pork roast in the slow cooker.

The amazing thing is that this roast is as simple as they come, one of the classic "throw it in and turn it on" meals that still manages to deliver old-fashioned flavor and comfort. To this day, anytime I want something done at my house, all I have to do is pick up a pork roast and I magically have a willing volunteer in my husband.

Pork roast

1 pound carrots, peeled and chopped

1 large onion, diced

6 to 8 medium potatoes, peeled and cubed

One 10.5-ounce can cream of mushroom soup

Place the roast in a slow cooker and add the vegetables. Pour the soup over all. Cook on low for 7 to 8 hours or high for 3 to 4 hours.

6 to 8 servings

squash casserole

choosing a favorite dish for my grandmother Lucy was not an easy thing to do because, honestly, Grandmama likes everything. There isn't a single thing you can't set down in front of her that she won't enjoy and thank you for cooking. She's easy to please and grateful for everything—a by-product of living through the lean years of the Depression and a childhood of sharecropping. But there are two things I make that set Grandmama's eyebrows raising, and that's my Lemon Bars (page 229) and my Squash Casserole.

Grandmama had squash plenty growing up. It was one of the vegetables grown in abundance in Lela's garden, but Lela didn't make many casseroles. Until she grew up, Grandmama had only had squash sautéed in water or a little bacon grease and then seasoned with salt, pepper, and a little sugar. For someone who loves the taste of squash in its purest form, having a good old-fashioned squash casserole is ooey-gooey heaven.

One of the things I like most about this dish is that it makes an 8 x 8-inch pan full. When homegrown squash is not available and I have to buy it at the grocery store, I've found that frozen squash is better than what is available in the produce section. The quality and size is more uniform and it is also much more economical.

4 cups sliced yellow squash

½ cup chopped onion

1½ cups water

4 tablespoons (½ stick) butter, melted

1 sleeve buttery round crackers (such as Ritz)

1 cup shredded cheddar cheese

1 teaspoon salt

Black pepper to taste

¾ cup milk

2 eggs, beaten

2 tablespoons butter

Preheat the oven to 350°F. Put the squash, onion, and water in a large skillet. Place over medium heat and cook until the squash and onion are tender, 5 to 10 minutes. Drain well. Add the margarine and stir to melt it in.

In a medium bowl, crush the crackers and stir in the cheese. Add the salt and pepper. Stir half of the cracker mixture into the squash.

In a small bowl, mix together the milk and eggs. Pour into the squash mixture and stir well. Pour into a casserole dish. Top with the remaining crumb mixture and dot with the remaining butter. Bake for 25 to 30 minutes, until the top is browned.

8 servings

yellow cake with peanut butter icing

Red was my great-grandmother's sister. Her given name was Stella, but I took to calling her Red when I was just a girl because she insisted that her hair be dyed red at all times. She used to come and stay with my grandparents often, and I was pretty close to both her and my great-grandmother, whom we all called simply by her name, "Lela."

Red was a young one, having been born sixteen years after Lela in the modern year of 1918. Red and Lela were very close and I was their tagalong. Whenever Red was visiting, my mother would always be sure to take me by and allow me to spend a day or two with them. Their birthdays were one day apart, and Mama even started checking me out of school so that I could go take them gifts and be there for cake on the day they both celebrated (I still don't think my siblings know about this!).

Lela passed away in 1991, when I was seventeen. I didn't get to see Red nearly as much after that. She got in a "bad way," as folks say, and wasn't able to get out much. Six years went by, and I did see her some, but her health was declining and her birthday was coming up.

She had a daughter in California who wanted to visit, and it was silently understood that Red might not be with us for too much longer. Her daughter wanted to make a big event out of her birthday, so she rented a banquet hall at a hotel and invited a large crowd for a grand celebration.

As Red's daughter went about making plans for the party, she asked Red what kind of cake she wanted. Red, with a defiant streak to match her hair color, stated plainly, "Lucille makes my cake." Her daughter apparently had missed the tradition that had grown over the years of my grandmother making Stella's favorite cake for her birthday each year and Red growing ever fonder of it, looking forward to this fudgy peanut butter icing on her special day. So in the end, Red got her way.

I was going to college and living with my grandmother at this time (Lucille, Lela's daughter and Red's niece). Granddaddy had just passed away, so it was just Grandmama and me living together as "roomies."

The day of Red's party arrived, and I drove Grandmama the two hours to the hotel where the party was held. The two of us walked into this hotel lobby, to this fancy banquet hall with flowers and balloons, folks all dressed up, and Red there with a corsage.

Enter my grandmother carrying a glass 9 x 13-inch Pyrex dish with a Duncan Hines yellow cake and homemade peanut butter icing.

Red was thrilled. It was just what she wanted.

Red and Lela aren't really gone; neither is Granddaddy for that matter. They all still hang around us, and I know they can smell this icing and long for a bite each time I make it.

1 box yellow cake mix
1½ cups sugar
7 tablespoons milk
2 tablespoons shortening
2 tablespoons margarine
¼ teaspoon salt
1 teaspoon vanilla extract
½ cup creamy peanut butter

Prepare the cake mix according to the package directions, baking it in a 9 x 13-inch pan.

While the cake is cooling, combine the sugar, milk, shortening, margarine, and salt in a medium heavy saucepan. Bring to a rolling boil, stirring constantly to prevent scorching. Once it reaches a rolling boil, stop stirring and let boil for 1 to 2 minutes, or until it reaches the soft-ball stage. Remove from the heat and quickly stir in the vanilla and peanut butter. Beat until smooth and quickly spread onto the cake.

12 servings

a little something to take with ya

in my family, whenever we eat at one of my grandparents' houses we're always followed right to the door and handed a plate covered in tinfoil. Folks can't seem to bear you leaving empty-handed, so you get a plate for the road just in case you get hungry later. "Here ya go, honey, here's a little somethin' to take with ya."

I feel the same way, and so I just had to give you a little something extra at the end of this book. Here ya go, honey, here's a little somethin' to take with ya . . .

"There is nothing more pleasant in life than to pass on to others
what one has learned for oneself."
—Confucius

"Most folks are about as happy as they make up their minds to be."
—Abraham Lincoln

"It's not what you gather, but what you scatter that tells
what kind of life you have lived."
—Helen Walton

"Let no one ever come to you without leaving happier."
—Mother Teresa

"Each day when you wake up, you have a choice. You can have a good day
or you can have a bad one. So you might as well have a good one."
—Christy Jordan

acknowledgments

justifiably, the first round of thanks went to my readers back in the introduction, so here is the second wave, but certainly no less important.

I want to thank Linda Konner, my literary agent, for believing in me, guiding me, and backing me up every step of the way. Without you, I would have never known this book was even in me.

My wonderful publisher, HarperCollins, which put full faith behind this book and a considerable amount of manpower into promoting it. Special thanks go to my editor, Julia Cheiffetz, and her assistant, Katie Salisbury. The two of them have had such faith in this book from day one that I couldn't help but have a little faith, too. They also met me where I was and didn't try to change a single thing about me, bless their hearts for that! I would also like to give a shout-out to my extended team at William Morrow— Liate Stehlik, Lynn Grady, Seale Ballenger, Brianne Halverson, Tavia Kowalchuk, and Shawn Nicholls.

I want to thank Jennifer Davick, who is behind the camera on all of this book's photography. She's photographed famous people and places all over the world, but was still able to get a feel for who I was, what *Southern Plate* stood for, and she remained true to that warmth and nostalgia. She can perform miracles with food photography, and has the patience of Job with kids who just want to eat the cookies instead of posing with them. Your photos are beautiful and no one could have done this like you!

I had no idea what a food stylist was until I met Marian Cooper Cairnes, who is the Mary Poppins of all things food. This gal practically whistles while she works, too. She came in like a whirlwind and turned my granny's recipes into art. When she left, my kitchen was cleaner than when she came and I found *five* pounds of butter in my refrigerator. Marian, when I go into butter addiction rehab, I'm sending you the bill.

Jan Gautro did all of the gorgeous prop styling for the photos as well as the Christy styling for me. If it weren't for her, y'all would likely see me in all of these shots wearing tennis shoes and blue jeans. My daughter felt an instant kinship with her because of her curly hair and easy smile. Jan, you'll always be "that girl with the curly hair" to us! Thank you for being "my peeps" and for making sure there wasn't broccoli in between my teeth on the cover!

Tanner Latham, your writing is poetry but your Lego talents are even more impressive. Thank you for helping out with the shoots. We sure did enjoy having you here and Brady said you can come build with him anytime!

I'd also like to thank Heather Shull and Deborah Bray, who helped me juggle writing the book and my kids' schedules by stepping in whenever they could. I cannot imagine how I would have gotten this done without you!

My mother-in-law, Linda, drove over from Georgia countless times to fill my shoes when deadlines got tight. I want to thank her for giving so freely of her time and my father-in-law, Rick, for sharing her, even if he did insist we send her back each time.

My husband, Ricky, for not rolling his eyes at yet another harebrained venture when I called in June of 2008 and said, "You know, I bet if I bought my own Web site and started a blog, I could get four or five hundred readers . . ." Ricky, I think it's safe to say I followed through on this one.

To my parents, for always believing in me. Thank you to my daddy, for being a man of integrity, and to my mama, for being the person I still hope to be when I grow up. I can't imagine a better inspiration.

To all of my dear friends who continue to support me: It's nice to feel as if I'm kind of normal at times, and surrounding yourself with folks as crazy as you sure does help!

Most important, I'd like to thank my two wonderful children, Brady and Katy Rose. My greatest dream came true when I became a mother, and you've filled my heart and my life with more joy than I could ever express. With you in my life, I can't help but greet each day with a song. My fondest wish is for you to have children when you grow up because only then will you be able to understand how very much your Mama loves you. When you do, be sure you cook all of these recipes for them, and tell them about those who came before. Never forget your root system; it's what keeps you growing straight.

~sighs~

I still miss my Granddaddy.

appendix

measurements and substitutions chart

Liquid Measures

1 gal = 4 qt = 8 pt = 16 cups = 128 fl oz
½ gal = 2 qt = 4 pt = 8 cups = 64 fl oz
¼ gal = 1 qt = 2 pt = 4 cups = 32 fl oz
½ qt = 1 pt = 2 cups = 16 fl oz
¼ qt = ½ pt = 1 cup = 8 fl oz

Dry Measures

1 cup = 16 Tbsp = 48 tsp = 250ml
¾ cup = 12 Tbsp = 36 tsp = 175ml
⅔ cup = 10⅔ Tbsp = 32 tsp = 150ml
½ cup = 8 Tbsp = 24 tsp = 125ml
⅓ cup = 5⅓ Tbsp = 16 tsp = 75ml
¼ cup = 4 Tbsp = 12 tsp = 50ml
⅛ cup = 2 Tbsp = 6 tsp = 30ml
1 Tbsp = 3 tsp = 15ml

Dash or Pinch or Speck = less than ⅛ tsp

Quickies

1 fl oz = 30 ml
1 oz = 28.35 g
1 lb = 16 oz (454 g)
1 kg = 2.2 lb
1 quart = 2 pints

U.S.	Canadian
¼ tsp	1.25 mL
½ tsp	2.5 mL
1 tsp	5 mL
1 Tbl	15 mL
¼ cup	50 mL
⅓ cup	75 mL
½ cup	125 mL
⅔ cup	150 mL
¾ cup	175 mL
1 cup	250 mL
1 quart	1 liter

Recipe Abbreviations

Cup = c or C
Fluid = fl
Gallon = gal
Ounce = oz
Package = pkg
Pint = pt
Pound = lb or #
Quart = qt
Square = sq
Tablespoon = T or Tbl
    or TBSP or TBS
Teaspoon = t or tsp

*Some measurements were rounded

Fahrenheit (°F) to Celcius (°C)

$°C = (°F − 32) \times 5/9$

Fahrenheit	Celcius
32°F	0°C
40°F	4°C
140°F	60°C
150°F	65°C
160°F	70°C
225°F	107°C
250°F	121°C
275°F	135°C
300°F	150°C
325°F	165°C
350°F	177°C
375°F	190°C
400°F	205°C
425°F	220°C
450°F	230°C
475°F	245°C
500°F	260°C

OVEN TEMPERATURES

WARMING: 200°F
VERY SLOW: 250°F–275°F
SLOW: 300°F–325°F
MODERATE: 350°F–375°F
HOT: 400°F–425°F
VERY HOT: 450°F–475°F

to make your own buttermilk:

Add 1 tablespoon lemon juice or white vinegar
to
1 cup whole milk.
Let sit for 5 minutes before using.

to make your own self-rising flour:

Add 1½ teaspoons baking powder
and
½ teaspoon salt
for *each* cup of all-purpose flour.

index

Note: Page references in *italics* refer to photographs.